C000229095

BENELUX

LOCOMOTIVES AND COACHING STOCK

THIRD EDITION

The complete guide to all Locomotives and
Coaching Stock of SNCB/NMBS, NS and CFL

David Haydock, Peter Fox & Brian Garvin

Published by Platform 5 Publishing Ltd., Wyvern House, Sark Road, Sheffield S2 4HG, England.

Printed in England by Alden Press, Osney Mead, Oxford OX2 0EF and BDC Printing Services Ltd., Slack Lane, Derby, DE3 3FL.

ISBN 1 872524 65-6.

© 1994 Platform 5 Publishing Ltd. All rights reserved. No part of this publication may be reproduced or transmitted in any form or by any means electronic, mechanical, photocopying, recording or otherwise, without the prior permission of the publisher.

2

SNCB/NMBS Class 2000 No. 2002 passes Lavaux with the 16.09 'Edelweiss' from Brussels to Roma on 15th June 1991.　　John C. Baker

CONTENTS

.

FRONT COVER PHOTOGRAPH: A pair of Belgian Class 51 diesels Nos. 5147/9 are seen at Tournai on 11th March 1994 with a cement train. On the left, in the platform, is an SNCF DMU.
Chris Wilson

BACK COVER PHOTOGRAPHS:

Top: NS Class 2200 No. 2327 leaves Terneuzen in January 1993 with a freight for Gent.
David Haydock

Bottom: CFL Class 3600 No. 3612 arrives at Pétange on 13th September 1990 with a commuter train from Luxembourg
C.L. Booth

INTRODUCTION

This book contains full details of all locomotives, multiple units and coaching stock of the state railways of the 'Benelux' countries, i.e. Belgium, the Netherlands and Luxembourg. Information is updated to Summer 1994.

Five years have passed since the second edition appeared. Since then, the SNCB and CFL fleets have not changed dramatically, but there has been a lot of movement in the Netherlands.

Belgium. The main change has been the insertion of centre-cars into "Break" units which have been repainted in an attractive new livery. This capacity increase has allowed the withdrawal of many old two-car EMUs by cascade. In 1995, the purchase of 80 ex SNCF "USI" coaches will allow the withdrawal of the last type K hauled coaches and more old EMUs. The diesel fleet has continued its contraction although many locos have been transferred to the "infrastructure" fleet.

The next few years will be much more eventful. The construction of a high-speed line will mobilise over 100 diesels meaning some will have to be bought or hired in, probably from NS and SNCF. Eurostar and TGV sets will start to appear and in 1996, the IC/IR network will be completely remodelled. Part of this plan involves the introduction of the new AM 96 EMUs which will allow further EMU withdrawals. A number of these units will be dual-voltage for operation into Luxembourg and France. By 1997, SNCB/NMBS should start to receive 70 dual-voltage electrics, which will begin to replace Class 22.

Netherlands. NS has at last caught up with its passenger traffic growth now that the last ICM, Class 1700 locos and double-deck suburban rakes are in service. More double-deck stock, in the form of IRM 'Regio Runner' EMUs, is now being delivered and power cars for double-deck suburban stock will arrive in 1996. These will free Class 1700 which will allow withdrawal of electric Classes 1100, 1200 and probably 1300. Indeed, the NS will then have a surplus of hauled stock! Delivery of Class 6400 diesels is almost complete, the last few arriving in the new red livery of the freight sector, NS Cargo. Reliability of this class is still suspect and is allowing Class 2200 to survive a little longer.

Luxembourg. The CFL network is now all electric except for a couple of short freight branches. The delivery of 22 Class 2000 EMUs has allowed service frequencies to be increased but diesels are still needed at peak times and because of the 3000 V d.c. — 25 kV a.c. break in Luxembourg. The **whole** of the present main line fleet is due to be replaced by 1997 as CFL is to order 30 dual-voltage locos in a common order together with SNCB/NMBS.

Goede Reis — Bon voyage - Good travelling!

GETTING THERE

By sea: Sealink offer a Harwich – Hoek van Holland (7 hour crossing) service: North Sea Ferries, Hull – Zeebrugge/Rotterdam (14 hrs); P & O, Ramsgate – Zeebrugge/Oostende (4 hrs) and a less frequent Felixtowe – Zeebrugge (5½ hrs). The fastest sea crossing is by P & O jetfoil from Ramsgate to Oostende (1½ hrs).

By air, there are flights are from all London airports and 16 regional airports, direct to Amsterdam's modern rail-served airport at Schiphol. Air UK offer many flights and British Midland are very price-competitive. Other operators are British Airways, KLM, Aer Lingus, Netherlands BV, Transavia and NLM. One can also fly to Brussels from many British airports.

ROVER TICKETS

Railway enthusiasts will find railrover tickets very useful. At the time of writing the following were available:
The Benelux Tourrail Card offers unlimited travel in Belgium (SNCB/NMBS), Luxembourg (CFL) and the Netherlands (NS). Prices: 5 days in a month - under 26 year olds BF 3030 (£60, over 26s BF 4040 (£80) 2nd, BF 6050 (£119) 1st. Obtainable from major Belgian and Luxembourg stations (not Netherlands).
BELGIUM SNCB/NMBS - Offers the 'B Tourrail' for any 5 days in a month. Price - BF 1980 (£39) 2nd, BF 2970 (£59) 1st. If you are under 26 the Eurodomino Junior Ticket is slightly cheaper at 3 days for £31, 5 days for £35, and 10 days for £65.
LUXEMBOURG CFL - Have a book of day tickets, buy 4 and get 5 tickets only 540 Lux Fr. (£10.74). Must be validated before start of first journey, valid to last station in Luxembourg. The 5 day Eurodomino is £17 (2nd).

NETHERLANDS NS - The Eurodomino 3 day ticket is £31 (2nd) £47 (1st) and £24 (junior 2nd), 5 days cost £51/£76/£38 respectively and 10 days cost £92/£137/£69. Alternatively in 1994 the NS issued a 'Zomertoer' pass (valid in June/July/August), and gave unlimited rail travel of 3 days out of 10 for 1 person - NLG 79 (2nd) 104 (1st), or 2 persons - NLG 109/149. The 'Zomertoer Plus' pass added Bus, Tram and Metro travel. 1 person - NLG 95/120 or 2 people -NLG 133/173. Also there is a 'Dagkaart' (Day Ticket) for NLG 58/87, and for an additional NLG 6.50 bus, tram and metro is added. For the under 18s the NS has a 'Tienertoer' pass which gives unlimited 2nd travel for 4 days out of 10 for NLG 56 (for additional NLG 14 bus, tram and metro is included). Valid during June/July/August and school holidays in Autumn, Christmas and Easter.

CLASS DIMENSIONS

Principal dimensions are given for each class in metric units. Standard abbreviations used in this book are:

km/h   kilometres per hour
kN   kilonewtons
kW   kilowatts

ACKNOWLEDGEMENTS

We would like to thank all who have helped with the writing of this book, especially Jan de Bruin, Rober Sturm, Max Delle and Michel Van Ussel, Messrs. Marcel Barthel and A. Ritz-Beckius at Luxembourg Depot, CFL, The public relations office of the SNCB/NMBS, also Messrs. G. Verhoeven (Département de Matériel) and L. Veriter (Salzinnes Works), the NS rolling stock department, also the Groupement Belge pour le Promotion et l'Exploitation Touristique du Transport Ferroviare (GTF), Liège and FEBELRAIL.

VEHICLE TYPE CODES FOR MULTIPLE UNITS AND HAULED STOCK

These are given in the continental system with the British codes in parentheses.

(1) CONTINENTAL SYSTEM:

f*   Bicycle Van (Dutch — bicycles = fietsen)
k*   Vehicle with with driving cab(s)
m*   Motor
s*   Driving Trailer
A   1st Class
B   2nd Class
D   Luggage, i.e., vehicle with luggage space and guard's compartment
R   Restaurant
K   Buffet or Kitchen
P   Post, i.e., vehicle with compartment(s) for mail (and guard)

* NS only.

Examples:

BD   Second Class with luggage/guard's compartment.
AB   Composite

Note – The continental system does not differentiate between open and compartment stock.

(2) BRITISH SYSTEM:

Coaching Stock codes are as used in our British Railways books e.g., F = first, S = second, C = composite, B = brake, O = open, K = side corridor with lavatory, so = semi-open.

The number of seats, lavatory compartments and washrooms are shown as nF/nS nT nW, e.g.: −/80 2T 2W has 80 second class seats, two lavatory compartments and two washrooms.

UIC HAULED STOCK NUMBERING SYSTEM

Loco-hauled coaches are numbered according to the UIC standard system as follows:

The number consists of four pairs of digits, which describe owner, speed, heating type etc., a three digit serial number and a check digit. The system is as follows:

(a) Digits 1 and 2 indicate the exchange condition.

50 Passenger coach. Internal use only
51 Passenger coach. International use
60 Departmental passenger coach
61 Special service hauled stock
71 Sleeping cars. International use

(b) Digits 3 and 4. These give the railway of origin, e.g.:

80 DB (German Federal Railways)
82 CFL (Chemins de Fer Luxembourgios)
84 NS (Netherlands Railways)
87 SNCF (French Railways)
88 SNCB (Belgian Railways)

(c) Digit 5. The fifth digit gives the class or type of vehicle.

1   First class
2   Second class
3   Composite
4   Couchette – first class
5   Couchette – second class or composite
6   Sleeping car – first class
7   Sleeping car – second class or composite
8   Special purpose vehicle
9   Postal or luggage van

(d) Digit 6. The sixth digit gives the number of compartments (or windows/seating bays in the case of open stock).

0   10 compartments or bays
1   11 compartments or bays
2   12 compartments or bays
3   six-wheeled carriage
4   four-wheeled carriage
5   Reserved
6   6 compartments or bays or double decker
7   7 compartments or bays
8   8 compartments or bays
9   9 compartments or bays
(d) Digits 7 and 8. These give the maximum speed and type of operation.

Digit 7:

0   120 km/h, electric heating
1   120 km/h, dual heating
2   120 km/h, steam heating (except for 29 – no heating)
3   121 – 140 km/h, electric heating
4/5 121 – 140 km/h, dual heating
6   121 – 140 km/h, steam heating (except for 69 – no heating)
7   141 – 160 km/h, electric heating
8   141 – 160 km/h, dual heating (except for 84 – steam, 89 – no heating)
9   Above 160 km/h

Digit 8 sometimes depends on digit 7, but in general:

0   All voltages
6   All voltages except 3000 V dc
7   1500 V d.c. or 50 Hz a.c.
8   3000 V dc
9   If digit 7 is 0,1,7 – 3000 V d.c. If digit 7 is 3,4,5 – 3000 V d.c. + 1000 V 16   Hz a.c.

Digits 9, 10 and 11. These give the serial number of the individual vehicle.
Digit 12. This gives the check digit. Multiply as follows:

Digit	1	2		3	4		5	6		7	8		9	10	11
x	2	1		2	1		2	1		2	1		2	1	2

Add all resultant digits and subtract the last number of the result from 10. This gives the check digit, example:

	5	0		8	4		2	9		3	7		2	4	8
x	2	1		2	1		2	1		2	1		2	1	2

$1+0+0 + 1+6+4 + 4+9 + 6+7 + 4+4+1+6 = 53$

Subtract 3 from 10 — check digit is 7.

BUILDERS

The following builder codes are used in this publication:

ABR	Ateliers Belges Réunis SA.
ACEC	SA Ateliers de Constructions Electriques de Charleroi.
AFB	Société Anglo-Franco-Belge des Ateliers de la Croyère.
Allan	N.V. Allan & Co.
Alsthom	Société Générale de Constructions Electriques et Mechaniques Alsthom.
ANF	Ateliers Construction du Nord de la France.
Arad	Astra, Arad, Romania.
BL	Brissonneau & Lotz.
BLC	Usines de Braine le Comte.
BN	La Brugeoise et Nivelles SA.
BND	La Brugeoise, Nicaise & Delcuve SA.
BRCW	The Birmingham Railway Carriage & Wagon Co. Ltd., Birmingham, England.
Beijnes	Koninklijke Fabriek van Rijtuigen en Spoorwagens JJ Beijnes NV.
Breda	Società Italiana Ernesto Breda per Construzzione Meccaniche, Milano, Italy.
CEM	Companie Electro Mecanique.
CF	Établissements Carel Fouché & Cie., Le Mans, France.
CFCF	Constructions Ferroviaires du Centre (Familleureux).
CWFM	SNCB Central Workshops, Mechelen.
Cockerill	SA Cockerill-Ougrée (Seraing).
De Dietrich	De Dietrich et cie., Reichshoffen.
Deutz	Klöckner, Humboldt, Deutz AG, Köln.
Donelli	Donelli SpA, Poviglio, Reggio, Emilia, Italy.
Duewag	Duewag Uerdingen.
EE	English Electric (Dick Kerr Works, Preston).
EIC	Entreprises Industrielles Charentaises, Aytré, La Rochelle, France (now BL).
FUF	Forges, Usines et Fonderies, Haine St. Pierre.
Fam.	Ateliers de Contruction de Familleureux, SA.
Fiat	Fiat, Torino,Italy.
GM	General Motors, USA.
Geismar	Société des Anciens Établissements L. Geismar, Colmar, France.
Germain	Ateliers Germain, Monceau.
Heemaf	Heemaf NV.
Henschel	Henschel und Sohn Gmbh, Kassel.
Jung	Arnold Jung Lokomotivfabrik Gmbh, Kirchen an der Sieg.
Krupp	Freid. Krupp, Essen.
MaK	Maschienenbau Kiel Gmbh, Kiel, Germany.
MTE	Société de Matériel de Traction Électrique, France.
Niv.	Les Ateliers de Construction Metallurgiques S.A., Nivelles, Belgium.
Oerlikon	Oerlikon, Switzerland.
Ragheno	SA Usines Ragheno.
Reggio	Officine Meccaniche Itialiane, Reggio d'Emilia, Italy.
SEM	Société d'Électricité et de Mécanique, Charleroi.
SEMG	Société d'Électricité et de Mécanique, Gent.
Schneider	Société des Forges et Ateliers du Creusot, Usines Schneider.
Smit	Smit, Slikkerveer.
Talbot	Waggonfabrik Talbot, Aachen.
Werkspoor	Werkspoor NV, Utrecht.
Westwaggon	Vereinigte Westdeutsche Waggonfabriken AG.

1. BELGIAN NATIONAL RAILWAYS (SNCB/NMBS)

Belgium is a country with two main languages The north of the country is Flemish speaking (Flemings) whilst the south is French speaking (Walloons). In addition to these main languages German is also spoken in a small part of the east. Flemish is a dialect of Dutch. Brussels is an exception being the only official dual-language area. We have compromised by using the terminology normally used in the various parts of the country. An exception is Brussels where the English version is used in preference to Brussel (Flemish) or Bruxelles (French).

Because of the language problem, Belgian National Railways uses the logo ⒷB rather than initials as these differ according to the language used! The Flemish use NMBS (Nationale Maatschappij der Belgische Spoorwegen) whilst the French use SNCB (Société Nationale des Chemins de Fer Belges).

NUMBERING SYSTEM

The SNCB list is quite straight forward. The present scheme dates from 01/01/71 and is as follows:

0001 – 1000	Electric multiple units. (Leading '0' not carried).
1001 – 2000	Electric locomotives. High speed range and multi-voltage.
2001 – 3000	Electric locomotives. Mixed traffic.
3001 – 4000	Eurostar rakes.
4001 – 5000	Diesel railcars.
5001 – 6000	Diesel locomotives. Higher power.
6001 – 7000	Diesel locomotives. Medium power.
7001 – 8000	Diesel shunting locomotives. Heavy duty.
8001 – 9000	Diesel shunting locomotives. Medium power.
9001 – 9999	Diesel shunting locomotives. Low power.

ORGANISATION, DEPOTS & STABLING POINTS

Since the first edition of this book appeared, there have been many reorganisations on Belgian Railways. These have eventually caught up with the traffic and motive power sections which have been reduced from eight areas to five regions. The list of stabling points is far from complete and does not include every station where the odd EMU may be stabled.

Central Region.

Depots: Brussels Midi/Zuid, Schaarbeek Diesel, Schaarbeek Electric.
Departmentals: Forest Vorst, Schaarbeek.
Stabling points: Brussels Midi/Zuid station, Ottignies.

North East Region.

Depots: Antwerpen Dam, Hasselt.
Departmentals: Antwerpen Oost, Leuven.
Stabling points: Aarschot, Antwerpen Centraal, Antwerpen Noord, Antwerpen Schijnpoort, Berchem, Leuven Station, Leuven Yard, Mechelen, Mol, Turnhout.

North West Region.

Depots: Kortrijk, Merelbeke, Oostende.
Departmentals: Brugge (also maintains some FSD shunters).
Stabling points: Aalst, Brugge, Denderleeuw, Dendermonde, De Panne, Gent St. Pieters, Geraardsbergen, Oudenaarde.

South East Region.

Depots: Kinkempois (Liège), Stockem.
Departmentals: Angleur, Arlon, Jemelle, Kinkempois, Visé.
Stabling points: Arlon, Bertrix, Gouvy, Huy, Jemelle, Liège Guillemins, Liers, Namur, Ronet, Stockem Yard, Virton, Welkenraedt.

South West Region.

Depots: Monceau (Charleroi), St. Ghislain.
Departmentals: Charleroi Sud, Mons.
Stabling points: Ath, Charleroi Sud, Châtelet, Mons, Tournai.

The SNCB has used codes for depots for many years dating back to the days of the telegraphic system. These codes are still in use today as official abbreviations. However on locomotives the allocation is normally stencilled on in full on the mainframe somewhere below the cab. EMUs and diesel railcars do not normally carry their allocations but somtimes the code will be found on them against repair data etc.

Note: (S) denotes stored and (D) denotes departmental service.

LIVERIES

The Belgian Railways have had a number of liveries in recent years. The old standard livery was green with a narrow yellow stripe for both electric and diesel locomotives, with a wider stripe for diesel shunters. The class 25.5 and the former Benelux EMUs were painted dark blue with a yellow stripe.

The main-line diesel locomotive fleet was being repainted in green with a much broader yellow stripe, but this then gave way to the current scheme of yellow with a green stripe. No distinction is made in this book between the two liveries. An exception is electric train-heat fitted diesels, which are painted blue and yellow. All new electric locomotives with the exception of Class 11 are now being painted blue with a yellow stripe and this livery is now being applied to older electric locos, which were originally blue with a larger area of yellow. Class 11 are painted in the Benelux livery which reflects their international use, as the upper half of the body is painted Bordeaux red, the new SNCB standard coach colour, whilst the lower part is painted yellow, the NS colour.

Diesel railcars are being repainted in blue, white and yellow, replacing the old yellow and red, whilst old EMUs are painted plain green. "Break" EMUs, originally painted in Bordeaux red, are coming out of works in a startling silver livery, lined in red/blue, and with a yellow frontal triangle. New EMUs are painted Bordeaux red, and certain old ones are being repainted in that colour, as are the type AM75/76/77 four-car units, which were originally painted grey and orange.

Coaching stock liveries are dealt with later.

WORKSHOPS

There are only two workshops for the general overhaul of locomotives and multiple units. However it should be stated that most of the main depots can undertake quite heavy repairs. A redistribution of responsiblities took place at the end of 1993. The main works are:

Mechelen: This works deals with all EMUs, diesel railcars and coaching stock.
Classes 15, 16, 22, 23, 25, 25.5 and 28.
Salzinnes: This works deals with all diesel and electric locomotives.

PLACE NAMES

Listed below are some of the towns and cities with their alternative rendering. Lille in France is included since the Flemish speakers do not use the word.
Fl. Flemish, Fr. French.

Usual Name	Alternative	Usual Name	Alternative
Aalst	Alost (Fr.)	Kortrijk	Courtrai (Fr.)
Arlon	Aarlen (Fl.)	Leuven	Louvain (Fr.)
Antwerpen	Anvers (Fr.)	Lille	Rijssel (Fl.)
Ath	Aat (Fl.)	Liège	Luik (Fl.)
Brugge	Bruges (Fr.)	Mechelen	Malines (Fr.)
Dendermonde	Termonde (Fr.)	Mons	Bergen (Fl.)
Gent	Gand (Fr.)	Namur	Namen (Fl.)
Geraardsbergen	Grammont (Fr.)	Oudenarde	Audenarde (Fr.)
Ieper	Yprès (Fr.)	Tournai	Doornik (Fl.)

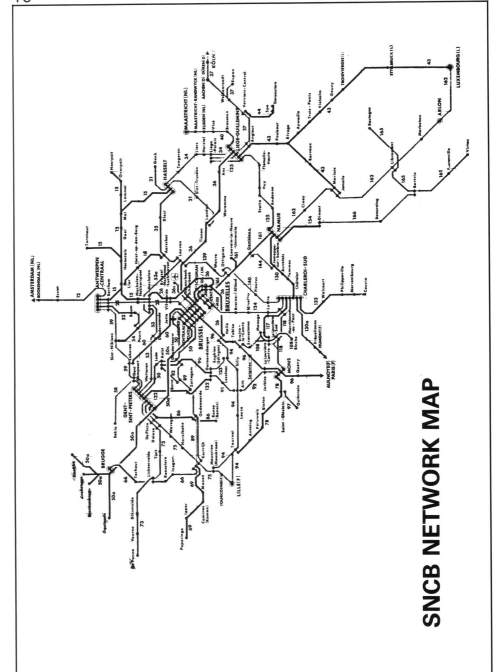

SNCB NETWORK MAP

ELECTRIC MULTIPLE UNITS

Belgian EMUs operate in fixed formations and therefore only unit numbers are quoted. All classes of EMU may work in multiple with one another except for types AM50/53, AM80/82/83, and type AM86, which may work with other members of the same type only. "Type" refers to the year in which the batch of units were ordered. Seating is 2 + 2 in first class and 2 + 3 in second class, except where stated otherwise. Livery is green unless otherwise stated.

TYPE AM50/53   2 CAR UNITS

These units are restricted to the Essen – Antwerpen – Brussels – Charleroi route (lines 12, 25, 27 and 124) where there are high platforms. To be withdrawn by 1996. 001 – 034 are type AM50 and 035 – 044 are type AM53.

AB + BD (DMCO – DMBSO).

Wheel Arrangement: A1 – 1A + A1 – 1A.
Built: 1950 (010 – 034) 1953/4 (035 – 044).
Builder-Mech. Parts: BND Energie (035 – 44).
Builder-Elec. Parts: ACEC, SEMG.
Traction Motors: 4 x 155 kW.
Accommodation: 30/60 1T + −/78 1T.
Weight: 47 + 45 tonnes.
Length over couplings: 22.672 + 22.420 m.
Max. Speed: 130 km/h.

Originally numbered 228.010 – 034.

010	FSRE	019	FSRE	030	FSRE	038	FSRE
011	FSRE	020	FSRE	031	FSRE	039	FSRE
013	FSRE	022	FSRE	032	FSRE	040	FSRE
014	FSRE	023	FSRE	033	FSRE	041	FSRE
015	FSRE	024	FSRE	034	FSRE	042	FSRE
016	FSRE	025	FSRE	035	FSRE	043	FSRE
017	FSRE	027	FSRE	036	FSRE	044	FSRE
018	FSRE	029	FSRE	037	FSRE		

TYPE AM54   2 CAR UNITS

Used on local trains, mainly on the Tournai – Namur line. Being withdrawn rapidly. Some units have been sold to Italian private operators ATCM in Modena and SATTI in Torino.

AB + BD (DMCO – DMBSO).

Wheel Arrangement: A1 – 1A + A1 – 1A.
Built: 1954 – 56.
Builder-Mech. Parts: 051 – 082 BN, 083 – 099 Rag, 100 – 128 Fam (AB), Germain (BD).
Builder-Elec. Parts: ACEC, SEMG.
Traction Motors: 4 X 155 kW.
Accommodation: 28/58 1T + −/85 1T
Weight: 43 + 42 tonnes.
Length over couplings: 22.640 + 22.640 m.
Max. Speed: 130 km/h.

Originally numbered 228.050 – 128.

053	FGH	083	FGH	102	FGH	114	FGH
060	FGH	090	FGH	104	FGH	119	FGH
063	FGH	092	FGH	106	FGH	121	FGH
067	FGH	094	FGH	107	FGH	122	FGH
077	FGH	095	FGH	108	FGH	124	FGH
081	FGH	096	FGH	113	FGH	125	FGH
082	FGH	100	FGH				

TYPE AM56 2 CAR UNITS

Post-war American influence is reflected in these units as they are finished off with Budd stainless steel panelling. These units are used on local trains mainly on the Tournai – Namur route.

AB + BD (DMCO – DMBSO).

Wheel Arrangement: A1 – 1A + A1 – 1A.
Built: 1956 – 7.
Builder-Mech. Parts: BN (under licence from Budd, Philadelphia, PA, USA).
Builder-Elec. Parts: ACEC, SEMG.
Traction Motors: 4 x 155 kW.
Accommodation: 28/58 1T + −/85 1T.
Weight: 40 + 39 tonnes.
Length over couplings: 22.985 + 22.985 m.
Max. Speed: 130 km/h.

Originally numbered 228.129 – 150.

129 U	FGH	136 U	FGH	141 U	FGH	146 U	FGH
130 U	FGH	137 U	FGH	142 U	FGH	147 U	FGH
132 U	FGH	138 U	FGH	143 U	FGH	148 U	FGH
133 U	FGH	139 U	FGH	144 U	FGH	149 U	FGH
134 U	FGH	140 U	FGH	145 U	FGH	150 U	FGH
135 U	FGH						

TYPE AM62/63/65 2 CAR UNITS

These units are in general use on local services over a wide area. 151 was converted into asynchronous-motored prototype 050 but will revert to standard in 1994.

ABD + B (DMBCO – DMSO).

Wheel Arrangement: A1 – 1A + A1 – 1A.
Built: 1962 – 1965. 151 – 210 are type AM62, 211 – 250 are type AM63 and 251 – 270 are type AM65.
Builder-Mech. Parts: BN, Rag, BLC, ABR, Germain, CWFM.
Builder-Elec. Parts: ACEC.
Traction Motors: 4 x 155 kW.
Accommodation: 28/48 1T + −/104 1T.
Weight: 49 + 50 tonnes.
Length over couplings: 23.592 + 23.713 m.
Max. Speed: 130 km/h.

Electro-pneumatic brakes. Disc brakes. Originally numbered 228.151 – 270.

151	FKR	177	LK	201	LK	225 R	LK
153	MKM	178 R	LK	202	LK	226	LK
154	MKM	179	LK	203	LK	227	FGH
155	MKM	180 R	LK	204	LK	228	FGH
156	MKM	181 R	LK	205 R	LK	229	FGH
157 R	MKM	182	LK	206	LK	230	FGH
158	MKM	183	LK	207	LK	231	FGH
159	MKM	184	LK	208 R	LK	232	FGH
160	MKM	185	LK	209	LK	233	FGH
161 R	MKM	186	LK	210 R	LK	234	FGH
162	MKM	187	LK	211	LK	235	FGH
163	MKM	188	LK	212 R	LK	236 R	FGH
164	MKM	189	LK	213	LK	237	FGH
165	MKM	190	LK	214 R	LK	238	FGH
166 R	MKM	191 R	LK	215	LK	239	FGH
167 R	LK	192 R	LK	216 R	LK	240	FGH
168	MKM	193	LK	217	LK	241	FGH
169	MKM	194	LK	218	LK	242 R	FGH
170	MKM	195 R	LK	219	LK	243 R	FGH
171	MKM	196	LK	220 R	LK	244	FGH
172	MKM	197	LK	221	LK	245 R	FGH
174	LK	198	LK	222	LK	246	FGH
175	LK	199	LK	223	LK	247	LK
176	LK	200	LK	224	LK	248 R	LK

249 R	LK	255	LK	261	LK	266	LK
250	LK	256	LK	262	LK	267	LK
251	LK	257	LK	263	LK	268	LK
252	LK	258	LK	264	LK	269 R	LK
253	LK	259	LK	265	LK	270 R	LK
254	LK	260	LK				

TYPE AM80/82/83 — 2 or 3 CAR UNITS

These are the latest generation of Belgian EMUs and feature thyristor control. They have interiors similar to M4 loco-hauled stock. Nicknamed ''break'' units. Automatic doors have an audible warning of closure. Pressure ventilation. MKM units are used on routes 161 and 162, NK units on routes 34, 75A, 78, 97, 112, 118, 125 and 130 and FSD units on routes 21, 21A, 36, 40, 50, 51, 51B and 161. New trailers with 2 + 2 second class seating are being inserted to make units up to 3 car sets. At the same time units are being repainted into a new silver livery.

B + ABD (DMSO – PDTBCO) or B + B + ABD (DMSO – TSO – PDTBCO).

Wheel Arrangement: Bo – Bo (+ 2 – 2) + 2 – 2.
Built: 1980 – 85. 301 – 335 are type AM80, 336 – 370 are type AM82 and 371 – 440 are type AM83.
Builder-Mech. Parts: BN.
Builder-Elec. Parts: ACEC.
Traction Motors: 4 x 310 kW.
Accommodation: – /99 1T + – /82 1T + 32/40 1T
Weight: 60 + 44 + 47 tonnes.
Length over couplings: 25.425 + 24.96 m + 25.425 m.
Max. Speed: 160 km/h.

Disc brakes. Electro-pneumatic and regenerative braking.
b Brecknell-Willis pantograph.
* Converted to three-car unit.

301 S	*	MKM	336 S	*	FHS	371 R		FKR	406 R		FKR
302 S	*	MKM	337 S	*	FHS	372 R		FKR	407 R		FKR
303 S	*	MKM	338 S	*	FHS	373 S	*	FKR	408 R	b	FKR
304 S	*	MKM	339 S	*	FHS	374 R		FKR	409 R		FKR
305 R		MKM	340 S	*	FHS	375 S	*	FKR	410 R		FKR
306 S	*	MKM	341 S	*	FHS	376 S	*	FKR	411 R		FKR
307 R		MKM	342 S	*	FHS	377 S	*	FKR	412 R		FKR
308 S	*	MKM	343 S	*	FHS	378 S	*	FKR	413 R		FKR
309 S	*	MKM	344 S	*	FHS	379 S	*	FKR	414 R		FKR
310 S	*	MKM	345 S	*	FHS	380 S	*	FKR	415 R	b	FKR
311 S	*	MKM	346 S	*	FHS	381 R		FKR	416 R		FKR
312 S	*	MKM	347 S	*	FHS	382 R		FKR	417 R		FKR
313 S	*	MKM	348 S	*	FHS	383 R		FKR	418 S	*	FKR
314 S	*	MKM	349 S	*	FHS	384 S	*	FKR	419 S	*	FKR
315 S	*	MKM	350 S	*	FHS	385 S	*	FKR	420 R	b	NK
316 S	*	MKM	351 S	*	FHS	386 S	*	FKR	421 R	b	NK
317 S	*	MKM	352 S	*	FHS	387 S	*	FKR	422 R		NK
318 S	*	MKM	353 S	*	FHS	388 R		FKR	423 R		NK
319 S	*	MKM	354 S	*	FHS	389 R		FKR	424 R	b	NK
320 S	*	MKM	355 S	*	FHS	390 S	*	FKR	425 S	*b	NK
321 S	*	MKM	356 S	*	FHS	391 S	*	FKR	426 S	*	NK
322 S	*	MKM	357 S	*	FHS	392 S	*	FKR	427 S	*	NK
323 S	*	MKM	358 R		FHS	393 R		FKR	428 S	*	NK
324 S	*	MKM	359 S	*	FHS	394 R		FKR	429 S	*	NK
325 S	*	MKM	360 S	*	FHS	395 R		FKR	430 S	*b	NK
326 S	*	MKM	361 S	*	FHS	396 R		FKR	431 S	*	NK
327 S	*	FHS	362 S	*	FHS	397 R		FKR	432 S	*	NK
328 S	*	FHS	363 R		FHS	398 R		FKR	433 S	*	NK
329 S	*	FHS	364 S	*	FHS	399 R		FKR	434 S	*	NK
330 R		FHS	365 S	*	FKR	400 R		FKR	435 S	*	NK
331 S	*	FHS	366 S	*	FKR	401 R		FKR	436 S	*	NK
332 S	*	FHS	367 S	*	FKR	402 R		FKR	437 S	*	NK
333 S	*	FHS	368 S	*	FKR	403 R		FKR	438 S	*	NK
334 S	*	FHS	369 S	*	FKR	404 R		FKR	439 S	*b	NK
335 S	*	FHS	370 S	*	FKR	405 R		FKR	440 S	*	NK

TYPE AM96   3 CAR UNITS

Three-car EMUs for InterCity services to be built in 3000 V d.c. only or 3000 V d.c./25 kV a.c.
50 Hz versions, the latter for services to Lille in France and Liège – Luxembourg. AM96 units will
be fully air-conditioned and fitted with Danish IC3 type "rubber-ring" cab ends to allow passage
between sets.

AD + B + B (DMF – SO – DTSO).

Wheel Arrangement: Bo – Bo + 2 – 2 + 2 – 2.
Built: 1995 – 1999.
Builder-Mech. Parts: BN.
Builder-Elec. Parts: ACEC.
Traction Motors:
Accommodation: 48/ – 1T + – /92 1T + – /80 1T.
Weight:
Length over couplings: 26.400 + 26.400 + 26.400 m.
Max. Speed: 160 km/h.

Dual-voltage sets:

441	454	467	479
442	455	468	480
443	456	469	481
444	457	470	482
445	458	471	483
446	459	472	484
447	460	473	485
448	461	474	486
449	462	475	487
450	463	476	488
451	464	477	489
452	465	478	490
453	466		

3000 V d.c. sets:

501	519	537	554
502	520	538	555
503	521	539	556
504	522	540	557
505	523	541	558
506	524	542	559
507	525	543	560
508	526	544	561
509	527	545	562
510	528	546	563
511	529	547	564
512	530	548	565
513	531	549	566
514	532	550	567
515	533	551	568
516	534	552	569
517	535	553	570
518	536		

TYPE AM70A (SABENA)   2-CAR UNITS

Exclusively used on Brussels Airport services for which they were built until the train service alterations of 1984 since when they have also turned up on Brussels area local services in rush hours!
Known as 'Sabena' or airport units they were originally numbered 851 – 856 and were renumbered
to allow for the possible building of more four-car sets. Previously in a distinctive blue livery, all
are now in standard red.

ABD + B (DMBCO – DMSO).

Wheel Arrangement: A1 – 1A + A1 – 1A.
Built: 1970 – 71.

Builder-Mech. Parts: Rag.
Builder-Elec. Parts: ACEC.
Traction Motors: 4 x 170 kW.
Accommodation: 32/12 + −/72 1T.
Total Weight: 52 + 52 tonnes.
Length over couplings: 23.592 + 23.713 m.
Max. Speed: 140 km/h.

Electro-pneumatic brakes. Disc brakes.

595 R	FSRE	597 R	FSRE	599 R	FSRE	600 R	FSRE
596 R	FSRE	598 R	FSRE				

TYPE AM66/70   2 CAR UNITS

ABD + B (DMBCO – DMSO).

Wheel Arrangement: A1 – 1A + A1 – 1A.
Built: 1966/70 – 71.
Builder-Mech. Parts: BN, Rag, BLC, ABR.
Builder-Elec. Parts: ACEC.
Traction Motors: 4 x 170 kW.
Accommodation: 28/48 + −/104 1T.
Weight: 52 + 56 tonnes.
Length over couplings: 23.592 + 23.713 m.
Max. Speed: 140 km/h.

Electro-pneumatic brakes. Disc brakes.
* – Fitted with Timken roller bearings.
Originally numbered 228.601 – 664.

601 R	FSRE	617 R	FSRE	633	*FSRE	649 R	*FSRE
602 R	FSRE	618 R	FSRE	634 R	*FSRE	650	*FSRE
603 R	FSRE	619 R	FSRE	635	*FSRE	651	*FSRE
604 R	FSRE	620 R	FSRE	636 R	*FSRE	652	*FSD
605	FSRE	621 R	FSRE	637 R	*FSRE	653	*FSD
606 R	FSRE	622 R	FSRE	638	*FSRE	654	*FSD
607 R	FSRE	623 R	FSRE	639 R	*FSRE	655	*FSD
608 R	FSRE	624	FSRE	640 R	*FSRE	657	*FSD
609 R	FSRE	625 R	FSRE	641	*FSRE	658	*FSD
610 R	FSRE	626 R	FSRE	642	*FSRE	659	*FSD
611 R	FSRE	627 R	FSRE	643	*FSRE	660 R	*FSD
612 R	FSRE	628	FSRE	644	*FSRE	661	*FSD
613 R	FSRE	629	FSRE	645 R	*FSRE	662	*FSD
614 R	FSRE	630 R	FSRE	646 R	*FSRE	663	*FSD
615 R	FSRE	631 R	*FSRE	647	*FSRE	664	*FSD
616 R	FSRE	632 R	*FSRE	648	*FSRE		

TYPE AM70Th   2 CAR UNITS

The 'Th' in the type classification denotes thyristor control, these being the first Belgian units so fitted. Timken roller bearings. Used on lines 34, 78, 97, 116, 117, 125 and 130.

ABD + B (DMBCO – DMSO).

Wheel Arrangement: A1 – 1A + A1 – 1A.
Built: 1971 – 72.
Builder-Mech. Parts: CWFM.
Builder-Elec. Parts: ACEC.
Traction Motors: 4 x 170 kW.
Accommodation: 28/48 + −/104 1T.
Weight: 53 + 56 tonnes.
Length over couplings: 23.529 + 23.713 m.
Max. Speed: 140 km/h.

Electro-pneumatic brakes. Disc brakes.

665	NK	667 R	NK	669 R	NK	671 R	NK
666	NK	668 R	NK	670 R	NK	672 R	NK

673 R NK |674 R NK |675   NK |676 R NK

TYPE AM73/74/78/79   2 CAR UNITS

These are the production series of thyristor-controlled units.

ABD + B (DMCO – DMSO).

Wheel Arrangement: A1 – 1A + A1 – 1A.
Built: 1972 – 80.
Builder-Mech. Parts: BN (707 – 730 CFCF).
Builder-Elec. Parts: ACEC.
Traction Motors: 4 x 170 kW.
Accommodation: 28/48 + –/102 1T.
Weight: 52 + 56 tonnes.
Length over couplings: 23.592 + 23.713 m.
Max. Speed: 140 km/h.

Electro-pneumatic brakes. Disc brakes.

677	NK	704 R	NK	731	FHS	757	FSD
678	NK	705 R	NK	732	FHS	758	FSD
679 R	NK	706	NK	733	FHS	759	FSD
680	NK	707 R	NK	734	FHS	760	FSD
681 R	NK	708 R	NK	735	FHS	761	FSD
682	NK	709 R	NK	736	FHS	762	FSD
683	NK	710 R	NK	737	FHS	763	FSD
684	NK	711	NK	738	FHS	764	FSD
685 R	NK	712 R	NK	739	FHS	765	FSD
686	NK	713 R	NK	740	FHS	766	FSD
687 R	NK	714 R	NK	741	FHS	767	FSD
688	NK	715	NK	742	FHS	768	FSD
689 R	NK	716 R	NK	743	FHS	769 R	FSD
690	NK	717 R	NK	744	FHS	770	FSD
691	NK	718	NK	745	FHS	771	FSD
692	NK	719 R	NK	746	FSD	772	FSD
693	NK	720	NK	747	FSD	773	FSD
694 R	NK	721 R	NK	748	FSD	774	FSD
695	NK	722 R	NK	749	FSD	775	FSD
696 R	NK	723 R	NK	750	FSD	776	FSD
697 R	NK	724 R	FHS	751	FSD	777	FSD
698	NK	725 R	FHS	752	FSD	778	FSD
699 R	NK	726 R	FHS	753	FSD	779	FSD
700 R	NK	727 R	FHS	754	FSD	780	FSD
701	NK	728 R	FHS	755	FSD	781	FSD
702 R	NK	729 R	FHS	756	FSD	782	FSD
703 R	NK	730	FHS				

TYPE AM75/76/77   4 CAR UNITS

These thyristor-controlled units are gangwayed within the sets only. Pantographs are fitted to only one of the motor coaches. Pressure ventilation. Used on lines 12, 25, 50, 57, 59, 60, 96, 97 and 124.

AD + B + B + B (DTBFO – PMSO – MSO – DTSO).

Wheel Arrangement: 2 – 2 + Bo – Bo + Bo – Bo + 2 – 2.
Built: 1975 – 1979.
Builder-Mech. Parts: BN.
Builder-Elec. Parts: ACEC.
Traction Motors: 8 x 170 kW.
Accommodation: 56/– 1T + –/100 1T + –/106 1T + –/96 1T.
Weight: 51 + 60 + 60 + 49 tonnes.
Length over couplings: 25.112 + 24.402 + 24.402 + 25.112 m.
Max. Speed: 140 km/h.
Advertising Livery: Blue with clouds - a discontinued advert for VTM television channel.

Electro-pneumatic brakes. Disc and tread brakes.

801 **R**	FSRE	812 **R**	FSRE	823 **R**	FSRE	834 **R**	FSRE
802 **R**	FSRE	813 **R**	FSRE	824 **R**	FSRE	835 **R**	FSRE
803 **R**	FSRE	814 **R**	FSRE	825 **R**	FSRE	836 **R**	FSRE
804 **R**	FSRE	815 **R**	FSRE	826 **R**	FSRE	837 **R**	FSRE
805 **R**	FSRE	816 **R**	FSRE	827 **R**	FSRE	838 **R**	FSRE
806 **R**	FSRE	817 **R**	FSRE	828 **R**	FSRE	839 **R**	FSRE
807 **R**	FSRE	818 **R**	FSRE	829 **R**	FSRE	840 **R**	FSRE
808 **A**	FSRE	819 **R**	FSRE	830 **R**	FSRE	841 **R**	FSRE
809 **R**	FSRE	820 **R**	FSRE	831 **R**	FSRE	842 **R**	FSRE
810 **R**	FSRE	821 **R**	FSRE	832 **R**	FSRE	843 **R**	FSRE
811 **R**	FSRE	822 **R**	FSRE	833 **R**	FSRE	844 **0**	FSRE

TYPE AM86/89   2 CAR UNITS

The latest in Belgian EMUs designed to replace some of the oldest in traffic. They were the first Belgian EMUs to feature 2 + 2 seating in second class. Another innovation is the use of polyester sides and front nose which are stuck onto the main body. They are designed for eventual one-person operation and rear-view mirrors are fitted which are flush with the side of the vehicle when not in use. They are officially known as Sprinters, but their unusual front end appearance has led to them being nicknamed "Snorkels". Used on lines 25, 27, 52, 59 and 124.

AB + B (MSO – DTCO).
Wheel Arrangement: Bo – Bo + 2 – 2.
Built: 1988 – 91.
Builder-Mech. Parts: BN.
Builder-Elec. Parts: ACEC.
Traction Motors: 4 x 172 kW type AE121N.
Accommodation: 40/48 1T + – /86.
Weight: 59 + 47 tonnes.
Length over couplings: 26.400 + 26.400 m.
Max. Speed: 120 km/h.
Electro-pneumatic brakes. Disc brakes.

901 **R**	FHS	914 **R**	FHS	927 **R**	FHS	940 **R**	FHS
902 **R**	FHS	915 **R**	FHS	928 **R**	FHS	941 **R**	FHS
903 **R**	FHS	916 **R**	FHS	929 **R**	FHS	942 **R**	FHS
904 **R**	FHS	917 **R**	FHS	930 **R**	FHS	943 **R**	FHS
905 **R**	FHS	918 **R**	FHS	931 **R**	FHS	944 **R**	FHS
906 **R**	FHS	919 **R**	FHS	932 **R**	FHS	945 **R**	FHS
907 **R**	FHS	920 **R**	FHS	933 **R**	FHS	946 **R**	FHS
908 **R**	FHS	921 **R**	FHS	934 **R**	FHS	947 **R**	FHS
909 **R**	FHS	922 **R**	FHS	935 **R**	FHS	948 **R**	FHS
910 **R**	FHS	923 **R**	FHS	936 **R**	FHS	949 **R**	FHS
911 **R**	FHS	924 **R**	FHS	937 **R**	FHS	950 **R**	FHS
912 **R**	FHS	925 **R**	FHS	938 **R**	FHS	951 **R**	FHS
913 **R**	FHS	926 **R**	FHS	939 **R**	FHS	952 **R**	FHS

TYPE AM54P   2 CAR UNITS

These units were converted at Mechelen Works from type AM54 during 1987/88. They replaced six older units converted from type 25 stock. These latest units have been designed to handle mail carried in containers which will be loaded into the coaches and have roller shutter doors. A total of 86 containers can be carried. Used all over the network.

D + D (2DMBP).
Wheel Arrangement: A1 – 1A + A1 – 1A.
Built: 1954 – 56.
Builder-Mech. Parts: See type AM54.
Builder-Elec. Parts: ACEC, SEMG.
Traction Motors: 4 x 155 kW.   **Length over couplings:** 22.985 + 22.985 m.
Weight: 44 + 42 tonnes.   **Max. Speed:** 130 km/h.

961 (080) **P**	NK	963 (109) **P**	NK	965 (117) **P**	NK	967 (118) **P**	NK
962 (085) **P**	NK	964 (086) **P**	NK	966 (123) **P**	NK	968 (074) **P**	NK
969 (091) **P**	NK	971 (128) **P**	NK	973 (120) **P**	NK	975 (111) **P**	NK
970 (093) **P**	NK	972 (084) **P**	NK	974 (110) **P**	NK		

ELECTRIC LOCOMOTIVES

Note: All electric locomotives are in the standard blue livery with yellow stripes unless stated otherwise. The standard voltage is 3000 V d.c.

CLASS 11   Bo – Bo

These dual voltage (1500/3000 V d.c.) locos are a development of class 21 but lower powered. They are used on the Brussels – Amsterdam service. The SNCB provides the locos for these push & pull Inter-City services and the NS provides the coaching stock. Originally planned to be numbered 1101 – 1112, the higher numbers were eventually decided on to avoid conflicting with the NS 1100 class. Otherwise the class is part of the new family of locos of classes 11, 12, 21 and 27. Thyristor control.

Built: 1985 – 6.
Builder-Mech. Parts: BN.
Builder-Elec. Parts: ACEC.
Traction Motors: 4 x LE622S frame mounted.
One Hour Rating: 3310 kW.   **Total Weight:** 85 tonnes.
Maximum Tractive Effort: 234 kN.   **Length over Buffers:** 18.65 m.
Driving Wheel Dia.: 1250 mm.   **Max. Speed:** 140 km/h.

Electro-pneumatic braking. Rheostatic braking.

1181 **B**	FBMZ	1184 **B**	FBMZ	1187 **B**	FBMZ	1190 **B**	FBMZ
1182 **B**	FBMZ	1185 **B**	FBMZ	1188 **B**	FBMZ	1191 **B**	FBMZ
1183 **B**	FBMZ	1186 **B**	FBMZ	1189 **B**	FBMZ	1192 **B**	FBMZ

CLASS 12   Bo – Bo

Introduced in 1986, this latest member of the new generation of electric locos is another dual voltage machine (3000 V d.c./25 kV a.c.) and is used on the Antwerpen – Mouscron – Lille IC services, Mons – Tournai – Lille passenger services and Gent – Lille freights. They also now work to Paris. Thyristor control.

Built: 1986.
Builder-Mech. Parts: BN.
Builder-Elec. Parts: ACEC.
Traction Motors: 4 x LE622S frame mounted.
One Hour Rating: 3310 kW.   **Total Weight:** 85 tonnes.
Maximum Tractive Effort: 234 kN.   **Length over Buffers:** 18.65 m.
Driving Wheel Dia.: 1250 mm.   **Max. Speed:** 160 km/h.

Electro-pneumatic braking. Rheostatic braking.

1201	FSD	1204	FSD	1207	FSD	1210	FSD
1202	FSD	1205	FSD	1208	FSD	1211	FSD
1203	FSD	1206	FSD	1209	FSD	1212	FSD

CLASS 15   Bo – Bo

These are triple voltage locos (1500/3000 V d.c., 25 kV a.c.) for through workings to the NS and SNCF systems. The class is used on EC/IC/TEE services Paris – Brussels – Amsterdam, but in 1988 they were banned from the NS, Class 25.5 being used instead between Brussels and Amsterdam. The pantograph at No. 1 end is for d.c. and that at No. 2 end is for a.c.

Built: 1962.
Builder-Mech. Parts: BN.
Builder-Elec. Parts: ACEC.
Traction Motors: 4 x ES541 frame mounted.
One Hour Rating: 2780 kW.   **Total Weight:** 77.7 tonnes.
Maximum Tractive Effort: 170 kN.   **Length over Buffers:** 17.75 m.
Driving Wheel Dia.: 1250 mm.   **Max. Speed:** 160 km/h.

Electro-pneumatic brakes. Originally numbered 150.001 – 003/011/012.

1501	FSD	1503	FSD	1504	FSD	1505	FSD
1502	FSD						

CLASS 16   Bo – Bo

When introduced these locos brought a bold new styling to the SNCB and an electric blue livery instead of the dark green then prevailing. These are true international locos and work on 1500/3000 V d.c., 15/25 kV a.c.. The main sphere of operation is Paris – Brussels/Liège . Köln and Oostende – Brussels – Köln with one train through to Dortmund. For a few years one member used to work through to Basel on a holiday train. No. 1 end has two pantographs, one for 15 kV a.c. and one for 1500/3000 V d.c. whilst No. 2 end has the 25 kV a.c. pantograph.

Built: 1966.
Builder-Mech. Parts: BN.
Builder-Elec. Parts: ACEC.
Traction Motors: 4 x ES541 frame mounted.
One Hour Rating: 2780 kW.   **Total Weight:** 82.6 tonnes.
Maximum Tractive Effort: 196 kN.   **Length over Buffers:** 16.65 m.
Driving Wheel Dia.: 1250 mm.   **Max. Speed:** 160 km/h.

Electro-pneumatic brakes. Originally numbered 160.001 – 004/021 – 024.

1601	FSD	1603	FSD	1605	FSD	1608	FSD
1602	FSD	1604	FSD	1606	FSD		

CLASS 18   C – C

These four voltage locos are in effect a more powerful version of the SNCF CC 40100 and feature the monomotor bogies which the French find so popular. The pantograph layout is No. 1 end 1500/3000 V d.c., No. 2 end two pantographs, one for 15 kV a.c. and one for 25 kV a.c. The Class operate mainly Paris – Brussels/Liège and some Oostende – Köln services.

Built: 1973.
Builder-Mech. Parts: BN.
Builder-Elec. Parts: Alsthom.
Traction Motors: 2 x TDQ662C1 frame mounted.
One Hour Rating: 4450 kW.   **Total Weight:** 113 tonnes.
Maximum Tractive Effort: 196 kN.   **Length over Buffers:** 22.08 m.
Driving Wheel Dia.: 1100 mm.   **Max. Speed:** 180 km/h.
Non-standard Livery: Light grey with unpainted ribbed stainless steel lower panel which has a yellow surround. Turquoise blue around cab windows and bodyside grilles.

Electro-pneumatic braking. Rheostatic braking.

1801 **N**	NK	1803 **N**	NK	1805 **N**	NK	1806 **N**	NK
1802 **N**	NK	1804 **N**	NK				

CLASS 20   Co – Co

These thyristor controlled locos are the most powerful on SNCB and have had a chequered career with varying defects over the years which now appear to have been ironed out. The main use is on the Oostende – Brussels – Luxembourg artery as well as Stockem – Antwerpen.

Built: 1975 – 77.
Builder-Mech. Parts: BN.
Builder-Elec. Parts: ACEC.
Traction Motors: 6 x LE772G frame mounted.
One Hour Rating: 5150 kW.   **Total Weight:** 110 tonnes.
Maximum Tractive Effort: 314 kN.   **Length over Buffers:** 19.50 m.
Driving Wheel Dia.: 1250 mm.   **Max. Speed:** 160 km/h.

Electro-pneumatic brakes. Separately excited rheostatic brakes.

2001	MKM	2007	MKM	2013	MKM	2019	MKM
2002	MKM	2008	MKM	2014	MKM	2021	MKM
2003	MKM	2009	MKM	2015	MKM	2022	MKM
2004	MKM	2010	MKM	2016	MKM	2023	MKM
2005	MKM	2011	MKM	2017	MKM	2024	MKM
2006	MKM	2012	MKM	2018	MKM	2025	MKM

CLASS 21   Bo – Bo

These are similar to class 27 but lower powered. Used on push-pull trains with M4 or M5 stock and freights.

Built: 1984 – 1987.
Builder-Mech. Parts: BN.
Builder-Elec. Parts: ACEC.
Traction Motors: 4 x LE622S frame mounted.

One Hour Rating: 3310 kW.	**Total Weight:** 84 tonnes.
Maximum Tractive Effort: 234 kN.	**Length over Buffers:** 18.65 m.
Driving Wheel Dia.: 1250 mm.	**Max. Speed:** 160 km/h.

Rheostatic brakes.
* Under conversion at Salzinnes to asynchronous-motored dual-voltage loco.

2101	FSD	2116	FSD	2131	FSD	2146	FSD
2102	FSD	2117	FSD	2132	FSD	2147	FSD
2103	FSD	2118	FSD	2133	FSD	2148	FSD
2104	FSD	2119	FSD	2134	FSD	2149	FSD
2105	FSD	2120	FSD	2135	FSD	2150	FSD
2106	FSD	2121	FSD	2136	FSD	2151	FNDM
2107	FSD	2122	FSD	2137	FSD	2152	FNDM
2108	FSD	2123	FSD	2138	FSD	2153	FNDM
2109 **A**	FSD	2124	FSD	2139	FSD	2154	FNDM
2110	FSD	2125	FSD	2140	FSD	2155	FNDM
2111	FSD	2126	FSD	2141	FSD	2156	FNDM
2112	FSD	2127	FSD	2142	FSD	2157	FNDM
2113	FSD	2128	FSD	2143	FSD	2158	FNDM
2114	FSD	2129	FSD	2144	FSD	2159	FNDM
2115	FSD	2130	*FSD	2145	FSD	2160	FNDM

CLASS 22   Bo – Bo

A general purpose locomotive found all over the network. 2239 – 2250 were originally dual voltage (1500/3000 V d.c.) but are now standard with the first batch.

Built: 1953 – 54.
Builder-Mech. Parts: Niv.
Builder-Elec. Parts: SEMG/ACEC.
Traction Motors: 4 x CF729 axle-hung.

One Hour Rating: 1880 kW.	**Total Weight:** 87 tonnes.
Maximum Tractive Effort: 196 kN.	**Length over Buffers:** 18.00 m.
Driving Wheel Dia.: 1262 mm.	**Max. Speed:** 130 km/h.

Originally numbered 122.001 – 038/201/212.

2201 **Y**	FGH	2214	FGH	2227	FGH	2239	FGH
2202 **Y**	FGH	2215	FGH	2228	FGH	2240	FGH
2203	FGH	2216	FGH	2229	FGH	2241	FGH
2204	FGH	2217 **Y**	FGH	2230	FGH	2242	FGH
2205	FGH	2218	FGH	2231	FGH	2243	FGH
2206	FGH	2220 **Y**	FGH	2232	FGH	2244	FGH
2207 **Y**	FGH	2221	FGH	2233	FGH	2245	FGH
2208	FGH	2222 **Y**	FGH	2234	FGH	2246	FGH
2209 **Y**	FGH	2223	FGH	2235	FGH	2247	FGH
2210	FGH	2224	FGH	2236	FGH	2248	FGH
2211 **Y**	FGH	2225	FGH	2237	FGH	2249	FGH
2212	FGH	2226	FGH	2238	FGH	2250	FGH
2213	FGH						

CLASS 23   Bo – Bo

Another mixed traffic loco at work all over the system. Fitted with regenerative brakes for freight work and can work in multiple with others of the same class and class 26.

Built: 1955 – 57.
Builder-Mech. Parts: Niv.

Builder-Elec. Parts: ACEC/SEMG.
Traction Motors: 4 x CF729 axle-hung.
One Hour Rating: 1880 kW.
Maximum Tractive Effort: 196 kN.
Driving Wheel Dia.: 1262 mm.
Total Weight: 93.3 tonnes.
Length over Buffers: 18.00 m.
Max. Speed: 130 km/h.

Regenerative braking.

Originally numbered 123.001 – 083.
* 2383 is fitted with special equipment for banking at Liège. It was renumbered 124.001 and then 2401 before becoming 2383.
§ Has side portholes on bottom of bodyside and ventilation grilles as on class 27.

2301	FKR	2322	FKR	2343	FKR	2364	FSD
2302 §	FKR	2323 Y	FKR	2344	FKR	2365	FSD
2303	FKR	2324	FKR	2345	FKR	2366	FSD
2304	FKR	2325	FKR	2346	FKR	2367 Y	FSD
2305	FKR	2326	FKR	2347	FKR	2368	FSD
2306	FKR	2327	FKR	2348	FKR	2369	FSD
2307	FKR	2328	FKR	2349	FKR	2370	FSD
2308	FKR	2329	FKR	2350	FKR	2371	FSD
2309	FKR	2330	FKR	2351	FSD	2372	FSD
2310	FKR	2331	FKR	2352	FSD	2373	FSD
2311	FKR	2332	FKR	2353	FSD	2374 Y	FSD
2312	FKR	2333	FKR	2354	FSD	2375	FSD
2313	FKR	2334	FKR	2355	FSD	2376	FSD
2314	FKR	2335	FKR	2356	FSD	2377	FSD
2315	FKR	2336	FKR	2357	FSD	2378	FSD
2316	FKR	2337	FKR	2358	FSD	2379	FSD
2317	FKR	2338	FKR	2359	FSD	2380 Y	FSD
2318	FKR	2339	FKR	2360	FSD	2381	FSD
2319	FKR	2340	FKR	2361	FSD	2382	FSD
2320	FKR	2341	FKR	2362	FSD	2383	*FSD
2321	FKR	2342	FKR	2363	FSD		

CLASS 25   Bo – Bo

This class are push-pull fitted for use on trains around Antwerpen using M2 stock. 2504 was rebuilt from 2557 (2521) in 1979.

Built: 1960 – 61.
Builder-Mech. Parts: BN.
Builder-Elec. Parts: ACEC/SEM.
Traction Motors: 4 x CF729 axle-hung.
One Hour Rating: 1880 kW.
Maximum Tractive Effort: 196 kN.
Driving Wheel Dia.: 1262 mm.
Total Weight: 84 tonnes.
Length over Buffers: 18.00 m.
Max. Speed: 130 km/h.

Originally numbered 125.001 – 014.

2501	FBMZ	2505	FBMZ	2509	FBMZ	2512	FBMZ
2502	FBMZ	2506	FBMZ	2510	FBMZ	2513	FBMZ
2503	FBMZ	2507	FBMZ	2511	FBMZ	2514	FBMZ
2504	FBMZ	2508	FBMZ				

CLASS 25.5   Bo – Bo

Formerly numbered 2515 – 22, these locos were modified in 1973/4 to dual voltage 1500/3000 V d.c. for working the push & pull Brussels – Amsterdam service for which they received an additional headlamp and a special dark blue livery. Note that only one pantograph is fitted. These locos have been replaced on these duties by class 11 but still work to Amsterdam on former Class 15 duties as they are fitted with Dutch ATP (automatic train protection). They are not compatible with the new Benelux push-pull stock. After an accident in 1979, 2557 and 2504 changed identities.

Built: 1960 – 61.
Builder-Mech. Parts: BN.
Builder-Elec. Parts: ACEC/SEM.
Traction Motors: 4 x CF729 axle-hung.

One Hour Rating: 1880 kW.   **Total Weight:** 85 tonnes.
Maximum Tractive Effort: 196 kN.   **Length over Buffers:** 18.00 m.
Driving Wheel Dia.: 1262 mm.   **Max. Speed:** 130 km/h.

Originally numbered 125.015 − 016, 140.001 − 006 (later 125.101 − 106).

2551 (2515) **X**	FNDM	2554 (2518) **X**	FNDM	2557 (2521) **X**	FNDM
2552 (2516) **X**	FNDM	2555 (2519) **X**	FNDM	2558 (2522) **X**	FNDM
2553 (2517) **X**	FNDM	2556 (2520) **X**	FNDM		

CLASS 26   B − B

These locos feature monomotor bogies by Schneider and have two gear ratios giving maximum speeds of 100/130 km/h. Seen all over Belgium, the class is fitted for multiple working with other members of the class and with class 23 for heavy freights.

Built: 1964 − 71.
Builder-Mech. Parts: BN.
Builder-Elec. Parts: ACEC.
Traction Motors: 2 x 2ES508 frame mounted.
One Hour Rating: 2580 kW.   **Total Weight:** 82.4 tonnes.
Maximum Tractive Effort: 235 kN.   **Length over Buffers:** 17.25 m.
Driving Wheel Dia.: 1150 mm.   **Max. Speed:** 130 km/h.

2601 − 20 were formerly originally 126.001 − 005, 126.101 − 130.

2601	FGH	2610	FGH	2620	FGH	2628	FGH
2602	FGH	2611	FGH	2621	FGH	2629	FGH
2603	FGH	2612 **Y**	FGH	2622	FGH	2630	FGH
2604	FGH	2613	FGH	2623 **Y**	FGH	2631	FGH
2605	FGH	2614	FGH	2624	FGH	2632	FGH
2606	FGH	2615	FGH	2625	FGH	2633	FGH
2607	FGH	2617	FGH	2626	FGH	2634	FGH
2608	FGH	2618	FGH	2627 **Y**	FGH	2635	FGH
2609	FGH	2619	FGH				

CLASS 27   Bo − Bo

Developed after experience with Class 20, these are the first of the 1980s generation of electric locomotives and heralded a new era, being more powerful than their predecessors. Chopper control. Flexicoil suspension. They are used throughout the network on both passenger and freight work.

Built: 1981 − 1984.
Builder-Mech. Parts: BN.
Builder-Elec. Parts: ACEC.
Traction Motors: 4 x LE921S frame mounted.
One Hour Rating: 4380 kW.   **Total Weight:** 85 tonnes.
Maximum Tractive Effort: 234 kN.   **Length over Buffers:** 18.65 m.
Driving Wheel Dia.: 1250 mm.   **Max. Speed:** 160 km/h.

Electro-pneumatic brakes. Rheostatic brakes.

2701	FSD	2716	FSD	2731	NK	2746	NK
2702	FSD	2717	FSD	2732	NK	2747	NK
2703	FSD	2718	FSD	2733	NK	2748	NK
2704	FSD	2719	FSD	2734	NK	2749	NK
2705	FSD	2720	FSD	2735	NK	2750	NK
2706	FSD	2721	NK	2736	NK	2751	NK
2707	FSD	2722	NK	2737	NK	2752	NK
2708	FSD	2723	NK	2738	NK	2753	NK
2709	FSD	2724	NK	2739	NK	2754	NK
2710	FSD	2725	NK	2740	NK	2755	NK
2711	FSD	2726	NK	2741	NK	2756	NK
2712	FSD	2727	NK	2742	NK	2757	NK
2713	FSD	2728	NK	2743	NK	2758	NK
2714	FSD	2729	NK	2744	NK	2759	NK
2715	FSD	2730	NK	2745	NK	2760	NK

CLASS 28 Bo – Bo

Formerly numbered 2001 – 2003, these locos became class 28 in 1973 and with the withdrawal of Class 29 they are now the oldest electric locos at work on the SNCB and are due for early withdrawal. They are relegated to light duties and can usually be found on pilot/e.c.s. duties between Forest and Brussels Midi. 2803 caught fire in 1991 and is used for spare parts.

Built: 1949.
Builder-Mech. Parts: BM.
Builder-Elec. Parts: ACEC/SEMG.
Traction Motors: 4 x CF729 axle-hung.
One Hour Rating: 1985 kW.
Maximum Tractive Effort: 196 kN.
Driving Wheel Dia.: 1262 mm.
Originally numbered 120.001 – 003.

Total Weight: 85 tonnes.
Length over Buffers: 17.18 m.
Max. Speed: 130 km/h.

2801	FBMZ	2802	FBMZ

EUROSTAR SETS

The Eurostar sets, formerly known as Trans-Manche Super Trains (TMSTs) are being delivered for the Channel Tunnel services between London and Paris and Brussels. They are based on the French TGV design concept, and the individual cars are numbered like French TGVs.

Each train consists of two 9-coach sets back-to-back with a power car at the outer end. All sets are articulated with an extra motor bogie on the coach next to the power car. Coaches are numbered R1 – R9 (and in traffic R10 – R18 in the second set). Coaches R18 – R10 are identical to R1 – R9.

Systems: 25 kV a.c. overhead, 3000 V d.c. overhead and 750 V d.c. third rail.
Built: 1992 – 3 by GEC Alsthom at various works.
Wheel Arrangement: Bo – Bo + Bo – 2 – 2 – 2 – 2 – 2 – 2 – 2 – 2 – 2
Traction Motors: 6
Accommodation: – + –/52 1T + –/60 1T + –/60 2T + –/60 1T + –/60 2T + kitchen/bar + 39/– 1T + 39/– 1T + 29/– 1T.
Length: 22.15 + 21.845 + (7 x 18.70) + 21.845 m.
Max. Speed: 300 km/h (187.5 mph).

Note: Only sets owned by SNCB/NMBS are shown in this list. A full list is published in the annual Platform 5 books 'British Railways Locomotives and Coaching Stock' and British Railways Pocket Book No. 3 – DMUs and Channel Tunnel Stock.

3101	E	FF	3731010	3731011	3731012	3731013	3731014	3731015	3731016	3731017	3731018	3731019
3102	E	FF	3731020	3731021	3731022	3731023	3731024	3731025	3731026	3731027	3731028	3731029
3103	E	FF	3731030	3731031	3731032	3731033	3731034	3731035	3731036	3731037	3731038	3731039
3104	E	FF	3731040	3731041	3731042	3731043	3731044	3731045	3731046	3731047	3731048	3731049
3105	E	FF	3731050	3731051	3731052	3731053	3731054	3731055	3731056	3731057	3731058	3731059
3106	E	FF	3731060	3731061	3731062	3731063	3731064	3731065	3731066	3731067	3731068	3731069
3107	E	FF	3731070	3731071	3731072	3731073	3731074	3731075	3731076	3731077	3731078	3731079
3108	E	FF	3731080	3731081	3731082	3731083	3731084	3731085	3731086	3731087	3731088	3731089

DIESEL RAILCARS
CLASS 44

Used on branch lines, these units can work with class 734 trailers. The FKR units work Aalst – Burst, and at weekends on Eeklo – Gent – Oudenaarde – Renaix, whilst those at MKM are used on the Virton – Libramont and Libramont – Dinant routes.

B (DMS).

Built: 1954.
Builder: Germain, rebuilt 1975 – 78 by CWFM.
Wheel Arrangement: B – 2.
Engine: 2 x GM 6V71N of 118 kW each at 1800 rpm.
Transmission: Hydraulic. Voith.

Accommodation: – /93 1T.
Total Weight: 54 tonnes.
Length over couplings: 23.80 m.
Max. Speed: 100 km/h.

Originally numbered 604.01 – 10.

4401 **W**	FKR	4404 **W**	FKR	4406 **D**	FKR	4408 **D**	MKM
4402 **D**	FKR	4405 **W**	FKR	4407 **D**	MKM	4410 **D**	MKM
4403 **W**	FKR						

CLASS 45

These units can work in multiple with or without class 734 trailers. They can be found on the Virton – Bertrix – Libramont and Dinant – Libramont routes.

B (DMS).

Built: 1954 – 55.
Builder: Germain, rebuilt 1974 – 78 by CWFM.
Wheel Arrangement: 1A – A1.
Engine: 2 x GM 6V71N of 118 kW each at 1800 rpm.
Transmission: Hydraulic. Voith.

Accommodation: – /93 1T.
Total Weight: 54 tonnes.
Length over couplings: 23.80 m.
Max. Speed: 100 km/h.

Originally numbered 605.01 – 10.

4501 **D**	MKM	4504 **D**	MKM	4507 **D**	MKM	4509 **D**	MKM
4502 **D**	MKM	4505 **D**	MKM	4508 **D**	MKM	4510 **D**	MKM
4503 **D**	MKM	4506 **W**	MKM				

CLASS 46

This class is withdrawn, but two have been kept as museum stock.

B (DMS).

Built: 1952.
Builder: Ragheno.
Wheel Arrangement: 1A – A1.
Engine: GM 6V71N of 118 kW each at 1800 rpm.
Transmission: Hydraulic. Voith.

Accommodation: – /74 1T.
Total Weight: 24 tonnes.
Length over couplings: 16.22 m.
Max. Speed: 100 km/h.

Originally numbered 554.01 – 10.

4601 **D**	4603 **D**

CLASS 734   TRAILER

Originally numbered 734.01 – 10, the original numbers are still carried and quoted in preference to the full UIC number. These trailers work as required with classes 44 and 45.

B (TS).
Built: 1955.
Builder: CWFM.
Accommodation: – /80 1T.

Total Weight: 17.45 tonnes.
Length over couplings: 16.11 m.
Max. Speed: 90 km/h.

UIC numbers are 50 88 27 29 580 – 589, with the end digit being one less than the end digit of the old number.

734.01 **D**	FKR	734.04 **D**	FKR	734.06 **D**	FKR	734.10 **D**	FKR
734.03 **D**	FKR	734.05 **D**	FKR	734.07 **D**	FKR		

DIESEL LOCOMOTIVES

Note: All diesel locomotives are in yellow and green livery except where stated otherwise.

CLASS 51   Co – Co

This class of mixed traffic locos is found all over the network except in the Liège and Luxembourg areas where class 55 is used. They are mostly used on freights but there are still some rush hour and summer sunday passenger trains from Brussels to De Panne and Ronse.

Built: 1961 – 63.
Builder-Mech. Parts: Cockerill.
Builder-Elec. Parts: ACEC/SEM.
Engine: Cockerill/Baldwin 10-608A of 1435 kW at 650 rpm.
Transmission: Electric. Six axle-hung traction motors.
Train Heating: Steam. Vapor OK4616. (· No boiler).
Weight in Full Working Order: 117 (113.2, 5154 – 93) tonnes.
Maximum Tractive Effort: 272 kN.   **Length over Buffers:** 20.160 m.
Driving Wheel Dia.: 1010 mm.   **Max. Speed:** 120 km/h.

Multiple working fitted.
§ Fitted with carriage lighting jumpers for use with type M1 push & pull trains.
Originally numbered 200.002 – 093.

No.		Depot	No.		Depot	No.		Depot	No.		Depot
5101		FSR	5123	·	LNC	5145	·	FHS	5168		FNDM
5102		FSR	5124		FKR	5146	§	LNC	5170	·	FNDM
5103	§	FSR	5125	·	FKR	5147		LNC	5171	·	FNDM
5104		FSR	5126	·	LNC	5148	§	LNC	5172	·	FNDM
5105		FSR	5127	·	FHS	5149		LNC	5173	·	FNDM
5106		FSR	5128	·	FKR	5150		LNC	5174	·	FNDM
5107		FKR	5129	·	FHS	5151	·	FHS	5175	·	FNDM
5108	§	FKR	5130	·	FHS	5152	·	FHS	5177	·	FNDM
5109		FKR	5131	· §	LNC	5153	·	FHS	5178	·	FNDM
5110	·	FKR	5132	·	FKR	5154	·	FNDM	5179	·	FHS
5111		FKR	5133	·	FHS	5155	·	FNDM	5180	·	FNDM
5112	·	FKR	5134	·	FKR	5156	·	FNDM	5181	·	FNDM
5113	·	FKR	5135	·	LNC	5157	·	FNDM	5182	·	FNDM
5114		FSR	5136	·	FHS	5158	·	FNDM	5183	·	FNDM
5115	·	FKR	5137	·	FHS	5159	·	FNDM	5184	·	FNDM
5116	·	FKR	5138	· §	FHS	5160	·	FNDM	5185	·	FHS
5117	·	LNC	5139	·	LNC	5162	·	FNDM	5186	·	FNDM
5118		FKR	5140	·	LNC	5163	·	FNDM	5187	·	FHS
5119	·	FKR	5141	·	FHS	5164	·	FNDM	5189	·	FNDM
5120	·	LNC	5142	·	FHS	5166	·	FNDM	5192	·	FHS
5121	·	LNC	5143	·	FHS	5167	·	FNDM	5193	·	FHS
5122		FSR	5144	·	FHS						

CLASS 52   Co – Co

Classes 52, 53 and 54 are part of a large European family of locomotives. The design originated as Nohab/GM and similar locomotives are found in Denmark (Classes MX and MY), Hungary (Class M61) and Norway (Class Di3). Class 52 can be found mainly on freight between Namur and Athus via Virton, but also on a return Bertrix – Namur passenger train Monday – Friday. After many complaints from crews new cabs have been fitted to all locos which substantially alter the appearance of the locos. Since the restructuring of passenger services several locos have lost their boilers and been reclassified to Class 53.

Built: 1955.
Builder-Mech. Parts: AFB.
Builder-Elec. Parts: GM.
Engine: GM 16-567C of 1265 kW at 835 rpm.
Transmission: Electric. 6 axle-hung traction motors.
Train Heating: Steam. Vapor OK4616. · No boiler.
Weight in Full Working Order: 108 tonnes.
Maximum Tractive Effort: 245 kN.   **Length over Buffers:** 18.850 m.
Driving Wheel Dia.: 1010 mm.   **Max. Speed:** 120 km/h.

Multiple working fitted.
Rheostatic braking.
The original 5201 – 13 were originally numbered 202.001 – 013.

5201	MKM	5211	MKM	5215 (5302)	* MKM
5202	MKM	5212	MKM	5216 (5317)	* MKM
5205	MKM	5213	MKM	5217 (5318)	* MKM
5209	MKM	5214 (5307)	* MKM		

CLASS 53   Co – Co

These are similar to class 52 but have no train heating. Similar freight use to class 52. Several class 52s lost their boilers and were renumbered to Class 53. All are fitted with new cabs.

Built: 1955.
Builder-Mech. Parts: AFB.
Builder-Elec. Parts: GM.
Engine: GM 16-567C of 1265 kW at 835 rpm.
Transmission: Electric. 6 axle-hung traction motors.
Train Heating: None.   **Weight in Full Working Order:** 106.6 tonnes.
Maximum Tractive Effort: 245 kN.   **Length over Buffers:** 18.850 m.
Driving Wheel Dia.: 1010 mm.   **Max. Speed:** 120 km/h.

Multiple working fitted.
Rheostatic braking.
The original 5301 – 19 were originally numbered 203.001 – 019.

5301	MKM	5308	MKM	5315	MKM
5302 (5203)	MKM	5309	MKM	5316	MKM
5303	MKM	5310	MKM	5317 (5207)	MKM
5304	MKM	5311	MKM	5318 (5208)	MKM
5305	MKM	5312	MKM	5319	MKM
5306	MKM	5313	MKM	5320 (5210)	MKM
5307 (5206)	MKM	5314	MKM		

CLASS 54   Co – Co

Similar to Class 52, but no rheostatic braking and an additional headlight. Similar use to Class 52.

Built: 1955 – 57.
Builder-Mech. Parts: AFB.
Builder-Elec. Parts: GM.
Engine: GM 16-567C of 1265 kW at 835 rpm.
Transmission: Electric. 6 axle-hung traction motors.
Train Heating: Steam. Vapor OK4616. · No boiler.
Weight in Full Working Order: 108 tonnes.
Maximum Tractive Effort: 245 kN.   **Length over Buffers:** 18.850 m.
Driving Wheel Dia.: 1010 mm.   **Max. Speed:** 120 km/h.
Multiple working fitted.
* Not fitted with new cabs and carries original number 204.004.
Originally numbered 204.001 – 007.

5401	FEO	5403	FEO	5404 **G** *	FEO	5407	·	FEO

CLASS 55   Co – Co

This class is based in the Liège area for freight. Those with electric heating are used on trains on the Liège – Luxembourg line and are painted in blue & yellow livery instead of the standard yellow & green.

Built: 1961 – 62.
Builder-Mech. Parts: BN.
Builder-Elec. Parts: ACEC/SEMG.
Engine: GM 16-567C of 1435 kW at 835 rpm.
Transmission: Electric. Six axle-hung traction motors.
Train Heating: Steam. Vapor OK4616. · No boiler.
Weight in Full Working Order: 110 tonnes.
Maximum Tractive Effort: 272 kN.   **Length over Buffers:** 19.550 m.

Driving Wheel Dia.: 1010 mm.　　**Max. Speed:** 120 km/h.

Multiple working fitted.
Rheostatic braking.
e – Electric heating fitted using an ACEC 300 kW alternator.
§ – Fitted with carriage lighting jumpers for use on M1 type push & pull trains.
Originally numbered 205.001 – 042.

5501		NK	5511		NK	5523 Y e	NK	5533	§	NK
5502	·	NK	5512	· §	NK	5524	· §	NK	5534	·	NK
5503	·	NK	5513		NK	5525	§	NK	5535		NK
5504	·	NK	5514		NK	5526		NK	5536		NK
5505 Y e	NK	5515 Y e	NK	5527	·	NK	5537	§	NK
5506		NK	5517	§	NK	5528		NK	5538	· §	NK
5507	·	NK	5518		NK	5529 Y e	NK	5539		NK
5508		NK	5519	§	NK	5530	·	NK	5540 Y e	NK
5509	·	NK	5520		NK	5531 Y e§	NK	5541	§	NK
5510 Y e	NK	5521	§	NK	5532	·	NK	5542 Y e	NK

CLASS 59　　　　　　　　　　　　　　Bo – Bo

These locos are used on freights around Gent and have been retained for use on high-speed line construction trains.
Built: 1954 – 55.
Builder-Mech. Parts: Cockerill/ BN/Niv.
Builder-Elec. Parts: ACEC.
Engine: Cockerill/Baldwin 608A of 1280 kW at 625 rpm.
Transmission: Electric. Four axle-hung traction motors.
Train Heating: None.　　**Weight in Full Working Order:** 87.2 tonnes.
Maximum Tractive Effort: 196 kN.　　**Length over Buffers:** 16.180 m.
Driving Wheel Dia.: 1118 mm.　　**Max. Speed:** 120 km/h.

Originally numbered 201.005 – 046.
5910 is a museum loco and carries number 201.010.

5905	FKR	5917	FKR	5939	FKR	5947	FKR
5910 G	FNDM	5926	FKR	5941	FKR	5950	FKR
5916	FKR	5936	FKR	5946	FKR		

CLASS 62　　　　　　　　　　　　　　Bo – Bo

These locos are used on mixed traffic duties. They are found on passenger work around Gent, Charleroi, Mons, Hasselt and Antwerpen. 6391 – 93 were built first as prototypes with flexicoil suspension, but now have standard bogies designed by BN. A few locos are already scrapped following accidents.

Built: 1961 – 66.
Builder-Mech. Parts: BN.
Builder-Elec. Parts: ACEC.
Engine: GM 12-567C of 1050 kW at 835 rpm.
Transmission: Electric. Four axle-hung traction motors.
Train Heating: Steam. Vapor OK4616. · No boiler.
Weight in Full Working Order: 78.6 tonnes.
Maximum Tractive Effort: 212 kN.　　**Length over Buffers:** 16.790 m.
Driving Wheel Dia.: 1010 mm.　　**Max. Speed:** 120 km/h.

Multiple working fitted.
§ Fitted with carriage lighting jumpers for M1 push & pull trains.
Originally numbered 212.101 – 133, 212.001 – 003.

6201	FKR	6211	FKR	6219	FKR	6228	FKR
6202	FKR	6212	FKR	6220	FKR	6229	FKR
6203	·	FKR	6213	FKR	6221	FKR	6230	FKR
6204	FKR	6214	FKR	6222	§	FKR	6231	§	LNC
6205	·	FKR	6215 Y ·	NK	6223	FKR	6233	FKR
6206	FKR	6216	FKR	6224	§	LNC	6234	§	LNC
6207	FKR	6217	· §	LNC	6225	FKR	6235	FKR
6210	·	FKR	6218	§	LNC	6227	·	FKR	6236	FKR

6237		FKR	6263	·	LNC	6288		LNC	6313		FKR
6238		FHS	6264		FKR	6289	§	NK	6314	·	LNC
6240		FHS	6266	·	LNC	6290		LNC	6315		FKR
6241		LNC	6267		FHS	6291		FHS	6316		FHS
6242	·	LNC	6268		FHS	6292		FKR	6317		FHS
6243	§	LNC	6269	·	LNC	6293		FKR	6318		FHS(S)
6244	·	LNC	6270	·	LNC	6294		FHS	6319	·	NK
6245		FHS	6271	§	LNC	6295		FHS	6320	·	LNC
6246		FHS	6272	·	LNC(S)	6296		FHS	6321	·	FHS
6247		FKR	6273	·	LNC	6297		FHS	6322		FKR
6248	§	LNC	6274	§	NK	6298		FHS	6323	· §	NK
6249	§	LNC	6275	· §	LNC(S)	6299		FHS	6324	§	NK
6250	·	LNC	6276	·	FKR(S)	6300	·	FKR	6325		NK
6251		FHS	6277		LNC	6301		FKR	6326		FHS
6252		FHS	6278		LNC	6302	·	FKR	6327	·	FHS
6253		FHS	6279		FHS	6303	·	NK	6328	·	NK
6254	·	LNC	6281		FHS	6304		FKR	6329	· §	NK
6255		FHS	6282		LNC	6305	·	FKR	6330		FHS
6256	§	FKR	6283		FHS	6306		FKR	6331	·	FHS
6257	·	LNC	6284		LNC	6307		FKR	6333		FKR
6258		LNC	6285		LNC	6309	·	NK	6391		FKR
6260	·	FHS	6286	·	LNC	6311		FKR	6392		FKR
6261		FHS	6287	·	LNC	6312	·	FKR	6393		FKR
6262	·	LNC									

CLASS 70   Bo – Bo

This class is used on trip freights around Antwerpen.

Built: 1954.
Builder-Mech. Parts: BM.
Builder-Elec. Parts: ACEC.
Engine: ABC 8DUS of 515 kW at 650 rpm. (§ Cockerill 6-cylinder of 570 kW. ABC 6DXC of 550 kW at 750 rpm*).
Transmission: Electric. Four axle-hung traction motors.
Train Heating: None.   **Weight in Full Working Order:** 85 tonnes.
Maximum Tractive Effort: 196 kN.   **Length over Buffers:** 12.150 m.
Driving Wheel Dia.: 1070 mm.   **Max. Speed:** 50 km/h.

Originally numbered 270.001 – 6.

7001	*	FNDM	7003		FNDM	7005		FNDM	7006		FNDM
7002	*	FNDM	7004	§	FNDM					

CLASS 71   B – B

Rebuilt from 6601 – 03 in 1980 at FAZ. Used for hump shunting duties in the departure yard at Antwerpen Noord, plus local trips. All fitted with automatic couplers.

Built: 1962 – 63.
Builder: ABR.
Engine: ABC 6DXC 100-750A of 662 kW at 750 rpm.
Transmission: Hydraulic. Voith L217.
Train Heating: None.   **Weight in Full Working Order:** 74 tonnes.
Maximum Tractive Effort: 197 kN.   **Length over Buffers:** 13.440 m.
Driving Wheel Dia.: 1010 mm.   **Max. Speed:** 50 km/h shunting/80 km/h main line.

Originally numbered 222.001 – 3.

7101	FNDM	7102	FNDM	7103	FNDM

CLASS 73   C

General purpose shunters, sometimes used on trip freights. Most FHS locos carry names painted on the cabside.

Built: 1965 – 67 (1973 – 74 7336 – 75, 1976 – 77 7376 – 95).
Builder: BN (ABR 7326 – 7335).

Engine: Cockerill 6TH695SA (6T240CO*§) of 550 kW at 950 rpm.
Transmission: Hydraulic. Voith L217u.
Train Heating: None.   **Weight in Full Working Order:** 56 tonnes.
Maximum Tractive Effort: 211 kN.   **Length over Buffers:** 11.170 (11.404*§) m.
Driving Wheel Dia.: 1262 mm.   **Max. Speed:** 60 km/h.

a Auto-couplers for shunting.
§ Multiple working fitted for use in hump yards.
7301 – 35 were originally numbered 273.001 – 035.

7301	LNC	7325		LNC	7349	*	NK	7373	*a FHS
7302	LNC	7326	§	LNC	7350	*	FKR	7374	* FHS
7303	LNC	7327	§	LNC	7351	*	FKR	7375	*a FHS
7304	LNC	7328	§	LNC	7352	*	FKR	7376	* FKR
7305	LNC	7329	§	LNC	7353	*	FKR	7377	* FKR
7306	LNC	7330	§	LNC	7354	*	FKR	7378	* FKR
7307	LNC	7331	§	LNC	7355	*	FKR	7379	* FKR
7308	LNC	7332	§	LNC	7356	*	FKR	7380	* FKR
7309	LNC	7333	§	LNC	7357	*a	FHS	7381	* NK
7310	LNC	7334	§	LNC	7358	*	FKR	7382	* NK
7311	LNC	7335	§	LNC	7359	*	FKR	7383	* NK
7312	LNC	7336	*	FHS	7360	*	LNC	7384	* NK
7313	LNC	7337	*	FKR	7361	*	LNC	7385	* NK
7314	LNC	7338	*	MKM	7362	*	LNC	7386	* FKR
7315	LNC	7339	*	MKM	7363	*	LNC	7387	* FKR
7316	LNC	7340	*	MKM	7364	*	LNC	7388	* FKR
7317	LNC	7341	*	MKM	7365	*a	FHS	7389	* FKR
7318	LNC	7342	*	MKM	7366	*	FHS	7390	* FKR
7319	LNC	7343	*	LNC	7367	*	LNC	7391	* FKR
7320	LNC	7344	*	LNC	7368	*	LNC	7392	* FKR
7321	LNC	7345	*	LNC	7369	*	LNC	7393	* FKR
7322	LNC	7346	*	LNC	7370	*	FHS	7394	* FKR
7323	LNC	7347	*	LNC	7371	*a	FHS	7395	* FKR
7324	LNC	7348	*	LNC	7372	*	FHS		

CLASS 74   C

Shunters used in pairs, radio controlled for hump shunting in Antwerpen Noord yard, or for work around the docks.

Built: 1977.
Builder: BN.
Engine: ABC 6DXS of 550 kW at 750 rpm.
Transmission: Hydraulic. Voith L217u.
Train Heating: None.   **Weight in Full Working Order:** 59 tonnes.
Maximum Tractive Effort: 196 kN.   **Length over Buffers:** 11.404 m.
Driving Wheel Dia.: 1262 mm.   **Max. Speed:** 60 km/h.

Multiple working within class and with Class 82.

7401	FNDM	7404	FNDM	7407	FNDM	7409	FNDM
7402	FNDM	7405	FNDM	7408	FNDM	7410	FNDM
7403	FNDM	7406	FNDM				

CLASS 75   B – B

Originally main-line locos of class 65, these were downgraded to shunters in 1982 – 83 when their steam boilers and water tanks were removed. They are now used for heavy trip working around Antwerpen Docks.

Built: 1965.
Builder: BN.
Engine: GM 12-567D-1 (two-stroke) of 1075 kW at 835 rpm.
Transmission: Hydraulic. Voith L216 rsb.
Train Heating: None.   **Weight in Full Working Order:** 79 tonnes.
Maximum Tractive Effort: 191 kN.   **Length over Buffers:** 16.790 m.
Driving Wheel Dia.: 1118 mm.   **Max. Speed:** 82 km/h shunting/120 km/h main line.
Originally numbered 203.001 – 006.

▲ Type AM56 stainless steel-bodied EMU No. 137 coupled to type AM66 No. 609 stands at Mouscron with the 16.56 to Charleroi Sud. *David Brown*

▼ Class 25 No. 2504 approaches Berchem hauling the 16.15 Antwerpen Centraal – Aarschot peak hour service formed of non push-pull type M2 coaching stock. *David Brown*

7501 (6501)	FNDM	7503 (6503)	FNDM(S)	7505 (6505)	FNDM
7502 (6502)	FNDM	7504 (6504)	FNDM	7506 (6506)	FNDM

CLASS 80   C

General purpose shunter used around Brussels. 8043 – 8069 have much larger fuel tanks than 8001 – 42. Many withdrawn locos have been sold abroad, particularly to Italian track maintenance firms. Very similar to DB Class 360.

Built: 1960 – 1963.
Builder: BN (ABR 8025 – 40).
Engine: Maybach GTO6A of 480 kW at 1400 rpm.
Transmission: Hydraulic. Voith L37z Ub.
Train Heating: None.   **Weight in Full Working Order:** 52 tonnes.
Maximum Tractive Effort: 173 kN.   **Length over Buffers:** 10.360 m.
Driving Wheel Dia.: 1262 mm.   **Max. Speed:** 30 km/h shunting/60 km/h main line.
§ Compressed air dryer for shunting Eurostar rakes at Forest depot.
Originally numbered 260.001 – 069.

8001	§	FSR	8025		FSR	8046	FSR	8061	FSR
8002	§	FSR	8027		FSR	8047	FSR	8062	FSR
8006		FSR	8031		FSR	8049	FSR	8063	FSR
8007		FSR	8032	§	FSR	8050	FSR	8064	FSR
8008		FSR	8033	§	FSR	8051	FSR	8065	FSR
8009		FSR	8034		FSR	8052	FSR	8066	FSR
8011		FSR	8035		FSR	8053	FKR	8067	FSR
8012		FSR	8037		FSR	8055	FSR	8068	FSR
8018		FSR	8040		FSR	8058	FSR	8069	FSR
8020	§	FSR	8045		FSR	8059	FSR		

CLASS 82   C

General purpose shunters, sometimes used for trip workings. FNDM multiple fitted locos are used in pairs for trips around Antwerpen Docks.

Built: 1965/6 8201 – 55; 1972/3 8256 – 75.
Builder: ABR (BN 8241 – 45).
Engine: ABC 6DXS of 480 kW at 750 rpm.
Transmission: Hydraulic. Voith L217u.
Train Heating: None.
Weight in Full Working Order: 57 (59 m, 56 s) tonnes.
Maximum Tractive Effort: 191 kN.   **Length over Buffers:** 11.170 (11.320 s) m.
Driving Wheel Dia.: 1262 mm.   **Max. Speed:** 60 km/h.

m Fitted for multiple working within class and with Class 74 around Antwerpen.
s Rebuilt in 1977 to a slave unit by the removal of the cab.
8201 – 55 were originally numbered 262.001 – 055.

8201	FSD	8220	FVY(D)	8239		NK	8258	m	FNDM
8202	FSD	8221	NK	8240		NK	8259	m	FNDM
8203	FVY	8222	NK	8241		FR(D)	8260	m	FNDM
8204	FSD	8223	NK	8242		FSD	8261	m	FNDM
8205	NK	8224	NK	8243		FSD	8262	m	FNDM
8206	FSD	8225	NK	8244		FSD	8263	m	FNDM
8207	FSD	8226	NK	8245		NK	8264	m	FNDM
8208	FSD	8227	NK	8246		FR(D)	8265	m	FNDM
8209	FSD	8228	NK	8247		FR(D)	8266	m	FNDM
8210	FSD	8229	NK	8248		NK	8267	m	FNDM
8211	FSD	8230	NK	8249		FSD	8268	m	FNDM
8212	NK	8231	NK	8250		FSD	8269	m	FNDM
8213	NK	8232	FR(D)	8251		FR(D)	8270	m	FNDM
8214	FR(D)	8233	FSD	8252		NK	8271	m	FNDM
8215	NK	8234	NK	8253		NK	8272	m	FNDM
8216	NK	8235	NK	8254		NK	8273	m	FNDM
8217	NK	8236	FR(D)	8255		NK	8274	m	FNDM
8218	NK	8237	NK	8256	m	FNDM	8275	sm	FNDM
8219	NK	8238	NK	8257	m	FNDM			

CLASS 84   C

General purpose shunters. 8461 – 70 were renumbered from 8526 – 8535. Most are likely to be withdrawn or transferred to the "infrastructure" pool for work on the LGV soon.

Built: 1962 – 64, 1959/60 reb 1968 – 79§.
Builders: ABR (BM §).
Engine: ABC 6DUS (6DXS§) of 405 kW at 680 rpm.
Transmission: Hydraulic. Voith L37u.
Train Heating: None.
Weight in Full Working Order: 55.8 (57.3§) tonnes.
Maximum Tractive Effort: 157 kN.   **Length over Buffers:** 10.650 (10.150*§) m.
Driving Wheel Dia.: 1262 mm.   **Max. Speed:** 30 km/h shunting/50 km/h main line.
Originally numbered 250.004 – 025, 250.101 – 135, 252.026 – 035.

8426	FKR(D)	8439	FGH(D)	8451	GNS(D)	8461	§	FNDM
8427	MGR(D)	8440	FGH(D)	8452	GNS(D)	8462	§	FNDM
8428	MGR(D)	8441	FGH(D)	8453	GNS(D)	8463	§	FNDM
8429	FKR(D)	8442	GNS(D)	8454	FLV(D)	8464	§	FNDM
8430	FKR(D)	8443	LNC(D)	8455	FHS(D)	8465	§	FNDM
8431	FKR(D)	8444	FNR(D)	8456	FHS(D)	8466	§	FNDM
8432	FKR(D)	8447	FNR(D)	8457	FSR(D)	8467	§	FNDM
8433	GNS(D)	8448	FNR(D)	8458	FSR(D)	8468	§	FNDM
8434	FR(D)	8449	LNC(D)	8459	FSR(D)	8469	§	FNDM
8435	FGH(D)	8450	LNC(D)	8460	FSR(D)	8470	§	FNDM
8437	FR(D)							

CLASS 85   C

Used for general purpose shunting around Antwerpen, plus Essen, Muizen and Mechelen works.

Built: 1956 – 57.
Builder: FUF.
Engine: ABC 6DXS of 405 kW at 680 rpm.
Transmission: Voith L37u.
Train Heating: None.   **Weight in Full Working Order:** 57.3 tonnes.
Maximum Tractive Effort: 157 kN.   **Length over Buffers:** 10.000 m.
Driving Wheel Dia.: 1262 mm.   **Max. Speed:** 30 km/h shunting/50 km/h main line.

Originally numbered 252.001 – 025.

8501	FNDM	8508	FNDM	8514	FNDM	8520	FNDM
8502	FNDM	8509	FNDM	8515	FNDM	8521	FNDM
8503	FNDM	8510	FNDM	8516	FNDM	8522	FNDM
8504	FNDM	8511	FNDM	8517	FNDM	8523	FNDM
8505	FNDM	8512	FNDM	8518	FNDM	8524	FNDM
8506	FNDM	8513	FNDM	8519	FNDM	8525	FNDM
8507	FNDM						

CLASS 91   B

This class was originally numbered 9001 – 60 and was rebuilt in the late 1970s with more powerful engines and in some cases lengthened frames (marked §) ready for automatic couplings! Many have been made spare by changes in freight workings and have been transferred to departmental use. Those in traffic stock are used for shunting at small stations and yards. Some are used as loco depot pilots.

Built: 1961 – 64.
Builders: Cockerill (9101 – 10), ABR (9111 – 9135), BN (9136 – 60).
Engine: GM 12V71N (two-stroke) of 245 kW at 1800 rpm.
Transmission: Hydraulic. Esco Power Twin Disc 11500 HS390.
Train Heating: None   **Weight in Full Working Order:** 33.8 (35§) tonnes.
Maximum Tractive Effort: 90 kN.   **Length over Buffers:** 6.625 m (8.055 m.§)
Driving Wheel Dia.: 920 mm.   **Max. Speed:** 35 km/h shunting/40 km/h main line.

Originally numbered 230.001 – 010/101 – 150.

9101	FGSP(D)	9102	FGSP(D)	9103	FGSP(D)	9104	(D)

▲ Type AM50 high platform unit No. 024 at Antwerpen Centraal on 6th August 1994. These units are scheduled for early withdrawal. *Peter Fox*

▼ Type AM54 No. 104 at Tournai on 11th March 1994. this is another class to be withdrawn. *Chris Wilson*

▲ Type AM63 No. 214, repainted in the now-standard Bordeaux red livery arrives at Ath with a service from Mons during November of 1989. *David Haydock*

▼ Type AM83 'break' unit No. 425 at Waremme on 6th August 1994 with the 16.23 Knokke – Maastricht. These units were delivered as 2-car units in red livery, but are being strengthened to 3-car units and repainted in the attractive silver, blue and red livery. *Peter Fox*

▲ Type AM73 No. 713 leaves Tournai on 11th March 1994 with the 09.18 to Charleroi Sud.
Alex Dasi-Sutton

▼ Type AM77 No. 844 at Roosendaal on 5th August 1994 with the 14.53 to Gent. This unit is
the last one to be painted in orange and grey livery.   *Peter Fox*

▲ Type AM86 'Snorkel' unit No. 918 approaches Anterpen Centraal on 1st June 1989.*Peter Fox*
▼ Postal unit 970 in sidings outside Antwerpen Centraal on 6th August 1994.   *Peter Fox*

▲ Class 11 No. 1187 in Benelux push-pull livery leaves Brussels Midi with the 17.15 Brussels – Amsterdam on 30th May 1989. *Peter Fox*

▼ Class 12 No. 1203 stands at Mouscron with the 14.28 Antwerpen – Lille on 11th March 1994. *Chris Wilson*

▲ Class 15 No. 1502 at Aulnoye on 28th April 1992.   *T.N. Hall*

▼ Class 16 No. 1608 runs past Waremme station on 6th August 1994 hauling EC46 'Alexander von Humboldt' the 09.07 Berlin Zoo – Brussels Zuid/Midi.   *Peter Fox*

▲ Class 18 No. 1803 stands at Liège Guillemins on 13th August 1990 with a Paris – Köln service which it has just taken over.   *Andrew Dyson*

▼ Class 21 No. 2143 near Tournai with a freight on 11th March 1990.   *Alex Dasi-Sutton*

▲ Class 22 No. 2216 arrives at Sint Niklaas on 5th August 1994 on the 16.41 ex-Mechelen formed of vintage type K stock. *Peter Fox*

▼ Class 23 No. 2334 stands at Tournai on 6th April 1990. *Bob Sweet*

▲ Class 25.5 No. 2554 with another member of the same class working an Amsterdam – Paris tram past Antwerpen Noorderdokken. *David Haydock*

▼ Class 27 No. 2723 at Brussels Zuid/Midi with a train of double-deck M5 stock. 30th May 1989. *Peter Fox*

▲ Class 28 No. 2802 was in ex-works condition when seen on an e.c.s. train at Brussels Zuid/Midi on 11th September 1990.   *C.L. Booth*

▼ DMU No. 4502 at Bertrix on 31st May 1989.   *Peter Fox*

3

▲ Class 53 No. 5301 runs light onto Ronet depot. *David Haydock*

▼ Belgian e.t.h.-fitted Class 55 No. 5542 in blue and yellow livery at Lorentzweiler in Luxembourg with the 09.08 Liège – Luxembourg. *John C. Baker*

▲ Class 59 No. 5905 on show at the Mariembourg festival of the CFV3V. *David Haydock*

▼ Class 73 No. 7361 shunting at Merelbeke in 1993. *David Haydock*

▲ Class 75 No. 7505.   *David Haydock*

▼ Class 80 No. 8033 at Brussels Midi/Zuid on 1st June 1989.   *Peter Fox*

46

▲ Class 85 No. 8525.　　　　　　　　　　　　　　　　*David Haydock*
▼ Class 91 No. 9118 at Tournai on 11th March 1994.　　　*Chris Wilson*

▲ Class 92 No. 9208 at Brussels Midi/Zuid.   *David Haydock*

▼ Type M2 driving trailer second No. 49202 leaves Antwerpen Centraal on 1st June 1989 with
the 15.09 to Neerpelt.   *Peter Fox*

▲ Type M4 brake open second No. 52933 at Liège on 30th May 1994.   *Peter Fox*

▼ Type I6 couchette No. 14608.   *David Haydock*

9105	(D)	9119	FSR(D)	9133	§LNC	9147	§NK
9106	(D)	9120	LNC	9134	(D)	9148	§MKM
9107	FNDM	9121	FSR(D)	9135	§MKM	9149	(D)
9108	(D)	9122	FMS(D)	9136	§FKR	9150	FWO(D)
9109	FKR	9123	FKR	9137	§MKM	9151	NK
9110	FKR	9124	FMS(D)	9138	§FGSP(D)	9152	FKR
9111	LNC	9125	(D)	9139	§FNDM	9153	MKM
9112	LNC	9126	§LNC	9140	LBC(D)	9154	FNR(D)
9113	LNC	9127	(D)	9141	FCR(D)	9155	§NK
9114	LNC	9128	FMS(D)	9142	FNR(D)	9156	§NK
9115	LNC	9129	§FNDM	9143	NK	9157	FNRM
9116	§(D)	9130	§LNC	9144	§LNC	9158	§NK
9117	LNC	9131	LNC	9145	MGR(D)	9159	§MKM
9118	LNC	9132	FKR	9146	§NK	9160	FKR

CLASS 92   C

This class is now wholly in departmental use and used by the permanent way department on ballast trains etc. The locos are often stabled in engineers depots.

Built: 1960.   **Engine:** SEM 6K113HS of 255 kW at 1300 rpm.
Builder: BN.   **Transmission:** Hydraulic. Voith L37u.
Train Heating: None.   **Weight in Full Working Order:** 50.5 tonnes.
Maximum Tractive Effort: 147 kN.   **Length over Buffers:** 10.40 m.
Driving Wheel Dia.: 1262 mm.   **Max. Speed:** 45 km/h.
Originally numbered 232.001 – 025.

9201	FKR(S)	9208	FFO(D)	9214	LNC(D)	9220	FFO(D)
9202	FFO(D)	9209	FKR(D)	9215	MGR(S)	9221	FFO(D)
9203	FGH(D)	9210	MGR(D)	9216	LNC(S)	9222	FHS(D)
9204	FNDM(S)	9211	MGR(D)	9217	FEO(D)	9223	FGH(D)
9205	FHS(D)	9212	FNDM(S)	9218	FKR(D)	9224	FEO(D)
9206	MGR(D)	9213	FEO(D)	9219	FNDM(D)	9225	FKR(D)
9207	FEO(D)						

SELF-PROPELLED DEPARTMENTAL STOCK

This series consists mainly of overhead line inspection units. Full details of these are not available. They are found in separate sheds belonging to the traction supply department.

ES100 SERIES

Built new 1947 – 49.

ES 101	FSR	ES 103	GNS	ES 105	NK	ES 106	FKR
ES 102	FSR	ES 104	FSR				

ES200 SERIES

Built new 1971 – 72.

ES 201	FCR	ES 204 **R**	FKR	ES 207 **R**	FMS	ES 210	FR
ES 202	FSR	ES 205	LL	ES 208	FLV	ES 211	FNR
ES 203	LJ	ES 206	GNS	ES 209	NK	ES 212	FSR

ES400 SERIES

Conversions from class 43 DMUs.

ES 401 (4307) FSR	ES 404 (4319) LL	ES 407 (4320) FLV	ES 410 (4315) FVS
ES 402 (4325) FMS	ES 405 (4326) GNS	ES 408 (4305) FHS	ES 411 (4325) FCR
ES 403 (4328) FTY	ES 406 (4306) FGSP	ES 409 (4309) FR	

ES4600/4900 SERIES

Converted from class 46/49 DMUs and not renumbered.

4612	FVS	4901	FVS	4911	FLV

Ⓑ

▲ Class 82 No. 8206 at Brugge on 26th June 1992.   *G.B. Wise*

▼ Class 84 No. 8426, now the first of the class remaining in traffic at Oostende on the same date.

G.B. Wise

HAULED COACHING STOCK

Numbering. All Belgian stock has the official UIC number painted on the side of the coach in the centre, and its 'old' number, duly crossed out, either on the bottom left-hand corner or on the end of the vehicle. All stock has an 'old' number, including new stock being delivered! Old numbers are used in this section, with a note on the UIC series in the class details.

Types. There are three basic categories of hauled stock in Belgium. 'I' stock is for international use and has 2 + 1 seating in open firsts, 2 + 2 seating in open seconds and 6 seats to both first and second class compartments. 'K' stock is old slam-door stock and has hopper windows (K1) or wind-down windows (K2/3). One line on which it is to be found is Namur – Dinant. 'M' stock is sliding door stock. M1/2/3 is old design with reduced height. M4 stock is more modern, having tinted windows and pressure ventilation. M5 stock is double-deck push-pull stock used around Brussels in the peak periods. Seating in 'K' and 'M' stock is 2 + 2 in first class and 2 + 3 in second class. It must be stated that comfort is extremely poor in most Belgian non-international coaching stock.

Liveries. Livery on K and M1/2/stock is plain green, whereas M4/5 stock have the new Bordeaux red livery. However, M2 stock is now being repainted in red livery, but no details are available as to which coaches have been so-painted. Similarly, new I6 and I10 stock is in orange livery with a white band. Older international stock has been repainted in this colour. Couchettes have a blue livery with a pink band. Livery codes are not shown in this section.

INTERNATIONAL STOCK

TYPE IO   CORRIDOR FIRST

Built: 1974. Stainless steel TEE stock.
Bogies: Y 28.
Accommodation: 45/– 2T 1W.
Heating: Air conditioned.
Computer Numbers: 61 88 1889 991 – 996/926 – 932.

Builder: .
Length over Buffers: 25.5 m.
Weight: 44 tonnes.
Max. Speed: 160 km/h.

| 131 **U** | 133 **U** | 135 **U** | 141 **U** | 143 **U** | 145 **U** | 146 **U** | 147 **U** |
| 132 **U** | 134 **U** | 136 **U** | 142 **U** | 144 **U** | | | |

TYPE IO   CORRIDOR SECOND

Built: 1974. Stainless steel TEE stock. Now declassiified.
Builder: .
Bogies: Y 28.
Accommodation: –/45 2T 1W.
Heating: Air conditioned.
Computer Numbers: 61 88 29 89 980 – 983.

Length over Buffers: 25.5 m.
Weight: 44 tonnes.
Max. Speed: 160 km/h.

| 151 **U** | 152 **U** | 153 **U** | 154 **U** | |

WAGONS LITS   RESTAURANT CAR

Built: 1925 – 7.
Bogies:
Accommodation: 56 (42§).
Heating: Electric.
Max. Speed: 160 km/h.
Computer Numbers: 61 88 88 70 014/017/ 08 70 019/ 88 70 023/4/6, 08 70 027.

Builder: Reggio (BRCW*).
Length over Buffers: 23.45 m.
Weight: tonnes.

| 2764 | 2855 | 2869 | 2971 | 2973 | 2976 | 2979 | |

WAGONS LITSPULLMAN ADMINISTRATION CAR

Built: 1926 for Flèche d'Or. Rebuilt for La Scala Opera tour and now used in Nostalgic Orient Express.
Builder: BRCW.
Bogies:
Accommodation: – .
Heating:
Max. Speed: 160 km/h.

Length over Buffers: 23.45 m.
Weight: tonnes.

4013 51 88 09 70 013-2

WAGONS LITS   PULLMAN CAR

Built: 1929 for Côte d'Azur.
Bogies:
Accommodation:
Heating:
Max. Speed: 160 km/h.

Builder: EIC.
Length over Buffers: 23.45 m.
Weight: tonnes.

4148	51 88 09 70 148-6	Bar/disco.
4151	61 88 09 70 151-8	Pullman bar ex 'Mistral'.
4159	51 88 09 70 159-3	Pullman bar.
4160	51 88 09 70 160-1	Lounge car.

WAGONS LITS   RESTAURANT CAR

Built: 1940 – 43.
Builder: Niv. (4203 – 15), Reggio (4230), Arad (4243/7).
Bogies: Pensylvania.
Accommodation: 48U.
Length over Buffers: 23.45 m.
Weight: 52.6 tonnes.
Heating: Coal with through electric wiring.
Max. Speed: 160 km/h.
Computer Numbers: 51 88 88 50 007/11 – 13/74/85/17.

| 4203 | 4212 | 4213 | 4215 | 4230 | 4243 | 4247 | |

WAGONS LITS   RESTAURANT CAR

Built: 1955 incorporating parts of damaged cars. Vestibule and outer doors at one end only.
Builder: Breda.
Bogies: Pensylvania.
Accommodation: 48U.
Length over Buffers: 23.45 m.
Weight: 52.6 tonnes.
Heating: Coal with through electric wiring.
Max. Speed: 160 km/h.
Computer Numbers: 61 88 88 70 265 – 269.

| 4265 | 4266 | 4267 | 4268 | 4269 | |

WAGONS LITS   SLEEPING CAR TYPE AB30

Built: 1955 – 6. Budd-patent stainless steel bodies.
Builder: CF (4530 – 43), Ansaldo (4554).
Bogies:
Accommodation: .
Heating: .
Length over Buffers: 24.00 m.
Weight: tonnes.
Max. Speed: 160 km/h.
Computer Numbers: 71 88 70 70 015/4/2/3/1.

| 4530 | 4531 | 4532 | 4543 | 4554 | |

WAGONS LITS   UNIVERSAL SLEEPING CAR

Built: 1957 as war reparations cars.
Builder: Hansa (4581 – 4599), Donauwörth (4602 – 17).
Bogies: .
Accommodation: .
Heating: .
Length over Buffers: 25.10 m.
Weight: tonnes.
Max. Speed: 160 km/h.
Computer Numbers: 51 88 06 70 001/3/6/8/011/2/9/022/5/8/031/2/5/7.

| 4581 | 4586 | 4591 | 4599 | 4605 | 4611 | 4615 | 4617 |
| 4583 | 4588 | 4592 | 4602 | 4608 | 4612 | | |

WAGONS LITS

Built: 1967.
Bogies: Minden-Deutz M4.
Accommodation: .
Heating: Air conditioned.
Computer Numbers: 71 88 72 70 615 – 619.

SLEEPING CAR TYPE MU

Builder: Donauwörth
Length over Buffers: 26.40 m.
Weight: 61 tonnes.
Max. Speed: 160 km/h.

| 4792 | 4793 | 4794 | 4795 | 4796 | |

WAGONS LITS

Built: 1974 – 75.
Bogies: Minden-Deutz M6.
Accommodation: .
Heating: Air conditioned.
Computer Numbers: 71 88 75 70 156 – 161.

SLEEPING CAR TYPE T2

Builder: .
Length over Buffers: 26.40 m.
Weight: 61 tonnes.
Max. Speed: 160 km/h.

| 5108 | 5109 | 5110 | 5151 | 5152 | 5153 | |

1XXXX SERIES INTERNATIONAL STOCK

TYPE I4   CORRIDOR FIRST

Built: 1966.
Bogies: Schlieren.
Accommodation: 54/ – 2T 1W.
Heating: Electric.
Computer Numbers: 51 88 1970 402 – 4/6/7.
Formerly used on Benelux push-pull service.

Builder: .
Length over Buffers: 25.38 m.
Weight: 49 tonnes.
Max. Speed: 160 km/h.

| 11301 | 11302 | 11303 | 11304 | 11305 | 11306 | |

TYPE I6   CORRIDOR FIRST

Built: 1977.
Bogies: Fiat Y0270.S.
Accommodation: 54/ – 2T.
Heating: Electric.
Computer Numbers: 61 88 19 70 601 – 620.

Builder: BN.
Length over Buffers: 26.40 m.
Weight: 43 tonnes.
Max. Speed: 160 km/h.

11601	11604	11607	11610	11613	11615	11617	11619
11602	11605	11608	11611	11614	11616	11618	11620
11603	11606	11609	11612				

TYPE I10   OPEN FIRST

Built: 1988.
Bogies: .
Accommodation: 66/ – 2T.
Heating: Electric .
Computer Numbers: 51 88 11 70 001 – 015.

Builder: BN.
Length over Buffers: 26.40 m.
Weight: 41 tonnes.
Max. Speed: 160/200 km/h.

| 11701 | 11703 | 11705 | 11707 | 11709 | 11711 | 11713 | 11715 |
| 11702 | 11704 | 11706 | 11708 | 11710 | 11712 | 11714 | |

TYPE I4   PROTOTYPE CORRIDOR SECOND

Built: 1961. Converted from composite.
Bogies: Schlieren 24.
Accommodation: – /54 2T.
Heating: Electric.
Computer Numbers: 51 88 29 70 402-5.

Builder: .
Length over Buffers: 24.085 m.
Weight: 44 tonnes.
Max. Speed: 160 km/h.

| 12302 | |

54

TYPE I4   CORRIDOR SECOND

Built: 1966. Converted from first.
Bogies: Schlieren 25.
Accommodation: −/54 2T.
Heating: Electric or dual
Computer Numbers: 51 88 29 80 403/4, 29 70 407 − 9, 29 80 410 − 8.

Builder: .
Length over Buffers: 25.38 m.
Weight: tonnes.
Max. Speed: 160 km/h.

12303 d	12305	12307	12309	12311 d	12313 d	12315 d	12317 d
12304 d	12306	12308	12310 d	12312 d	12314 d	12316 d	12318 d

TYPE I6   CORRIDOR SECOND

Built: 1977 − 78.
Bogies: Fiat Y0270.S.
Accommodation: −/66 2T 1W.
Heating: Electric.
Computer Numbers: 61 88 21 70 601 − 659.

Builder: BN.
Length over Buffers: 26.40 m.
Weight: 43 tonnes.
Max. Speed: 160 km/h.

Note: Some of these vehicles have been converted to couchettes and numbered in the 146XX series.

12601	12609	12616	12622	12631	12640	12647	12653
12603	12610	12617	12625	12634	12641	12648	12654
12604	12611	12618	12626	12635	12642	12650	12656
12605	12613	12619	12627	12636	12643	12651	12658
12607	12614	12620	12629	12638	12645	12652	12659
12608	12615	12621	12630				

TYPE I10   OPEN SECOND

Built: 1987 − 88.
Bogies: .
Accommodation: −/86 2T.
Weight: 41 tonnes. (42.5 tonnes 12746 − 80).
Heating: Electric. 12746 − 79 are air conditioned.
Computer Numbers: 51 88 21 − 70 001 − 045, 61 88 21 70 046 − 079.

Builder: BN.
Length over Buffers: 26.40 m.
Max. Speed: 160/200 km/h.

12701	12711	12721	12731	12741	12751	12761	12771
12702	12712	12722	12732	12742	12752	12762	12772
12703	12713	12723	12733	12743	12753	12763	12773
12704	12714	12724	12734	12744	12754	12764	12774
12705	12715	12725	12735	12745	12755	12765	12775
12706	12716	12726	12736	12746	12756	12766	12776
12707	12717	12727	12737	12747	12757	12767	12777
12708	12718	12728	12738	12748	12758	12768	12778
12709	12719	12729	12739	12749	12759	12769	12779
12710	12720	12730	12740	12750	12760	12770	

TYPE I10   RESTAURANT CAR

Built: 1988. Converted from second.
Bogies: .
Accommodation: −/86 2T.
Weight: tonnes.
Heating: Electric. Air conditioned.
Computer Numbers: 61 88 21 70 080.

Builder: BN.
Length over Buffers: 26.40 m.
Max. Speed: 200 km/h.

12780

TYPE I4   CORRIDOR COMPOSITE

Built: 1966.
Bogies: Schlieren 25.
Accommodation: 24/36 2T 2W.
Heating: Electric or dual.
Computer Numbers: 51 88 30 70 402, 39 70 403 − 410 & 50 88 30 70 411 − 417, 30 80 419 − 21.

Builder: BN.
Length over Buffers: 25.775 m.
Weight: 44 tonnes.
Max. Speed: 160 km/h.

b Formerly used on Benelux push-pull service.

k One compartment used for trolley service.

13201 bk	13204 bk	13207 bk	13210	13213	13215	13217	13219
13202 bk	13205 bk	13208 bk	13211	13214	13216	13218	13220
13203 bk	13206 bk	13209 k	13212				

TYPE I3   SECOND COUCHETTE

Built: 1960.
Bogies: Schlieren 24.
Accommodation: /72 (54 berths) 2T 1W.
Heating: Dual.
Computer Numbers: 51 88 59 80 301 – 329.

Builder: .
Length over Buffers: 23.344 m.
Weight: 45 tonnes.
Max. Speed: 160 km/h.

14001	14004	14006	14008	14010	14024	14027	14029
14002	14005	14007	14009				

TYPE I5   SECOND COUCHETTE

Built: 1967.
Bogies: Schlieren 25.
Accommodation: /60 (60 berths) 2T 3W.
Heating: Electric or dual.
Computer Numbers: 51 88 50 70 501 – 507, 50 80 509 – 25, 50 70 508/526 – 545.

Builder: .
Length over Buffers: 26.40 m.
Weight: 47 tonnes.
Max. Speed: 160 km/h.

14101 e	14107 e	14113 d	14119 d	14125 d	14531 e	14536 e	14541 e
14102 e	14508 e	14114 d	14120 d	14526 e	14532 e	14537 e	14542 e
14103 e	14109 d	14115 d	14121 d	14527 e	14533 e	14538 e	14543 e
14104 e	14110 d	14116 d	14122 d	14528 e	14534 e	14539 e	14544 e
14105 e	14111 d	14117 d	14123 d	14529 e	14535 e	14540 e	14545 e
14106 d	14112 d	14118 d	14124 d	14530 e			

TYPE I6   SECOND COUCHETTE

Built: 1977 – 78. Converted from corridor second.
Builder: BN.
Bogies: Fiat YO270.S.
Accommodation: – /66 (66 berths) 2T 1W.
Heating: Electric.
Computer Numbers: 61 88 50 70 601 – 615.

Length over Buffers: 26.40 m.
Weight: tonnes.
Max. Speed: 160 km/h.

14601	14603	14605	14607	14609	14611	14613	14615
14602	14604	14606	14608	14610	14612	14614	

TYPE ID   BRAKE VAN

Built: 1939.
Bogies: Pensylvania.
Accommodation: 1T.
Heating: Dual.
Computer Numbers: 51 88 95 40 914/5/7.

Builder: .
Length over Buffers: 16.16 m.
Weight: 37 tonnes.
Max. Speed: 140 km/h.

17101	17102	17104	

TYPE ID   BRAKE VAN

Built: 1978.
Bogies: Fiat YO 332.
Accommodation: .
Heating: Electric.
Computer Numbers: 51 88 95 70 901 – 934.

Builder: .
Length over Buffers: 26.40 m.
Weight: 39 tonnes.
Max. Speed: 160 km/h.

17401	17405	17411	17417	17420	17425	17428	17432
17402	17406	17412	17418	17421	17426	17429	17433
17403	17407	17413	17419	17424	17427	17431	17434
17404	17408	17414					

EXHIBITION VEHICLES

No details except that 17815 is a generator.
Computer Numbers: 60 88 99 40 021 – 035.

17801	17803	17805	17807	17808	17809	17810	17815
17802	17804	17806					

TYPE I1   BAR

Built: 1933. Ex 12248.
Bogies: Schlieren 27.
Accommodation: Nil.
Heating: Electric with through steam pipe.
Computer Number: 51 88 89 80 001-8.

Builder: .
Length over Buffers: 22.30 m.
Weight: 45 tonnes.
Max. Speed: 160 km/h.

17816	17817	17901

TYPE I6   BAR

Built: 1978.
Bogies: Fiat 31.
Accommodation: Nil.
Heating: Electric. Air conditioned.
Computer Number: 61 88 89 70 002-6.

Builder: .
Length over Buffers: 26.40 m.
Weight: 48 tonnes.
Max. Speed: 160 km/h.

17902

2XXXX SERIES TYPE K STOCK

TYPE K1   OPEN FIRST

Built: 1933 – 34.
Bogies: Pensylvania.
Accommodation: 70/– 1T.
Heating: Electric.
Computer Numbers: 50 88 18 40 001 – 123. Some of those shown now withdrawn.

Builder: .
Length over Buffers: 23.32 m.
Weight: 43.1 tonnes.
Max. Speed: 140 km/h.

21005	21008	21015	21023	21026	21030	21038	21123
21007	21012	21017	21024	21029			

TYPE K3   OPEN SECOND

Built: 1956 – 58.
Bogies: Schlieren.
Accommodation: – /108 1T.
Heating: Dual.
Computer Numbers: 50 88 21 48 300 – 399. (Note: last digit one less than SNCB number.)

Builder:
Length over Buffers: 23.22 m.
Weight: 35.7 tonnes.
Max. Speed: 140 km/h.

22401	22413	22425	22436	22450	22469	22479	22492
22403	22414	22426	22438	22451	22471	22480	22495
22404	22418	22429	22439	22455	22472	22483	22496
22407	22419	22430	22441	22456	22473	22484	22497
22408	22420	22432	22442	22458	22474	22488	22498
22410	22421	22433	22444	22460	22476	22490	22499
22411	22423	22434	22445	22462	22477	22491	22500
22412	22424	22435	22446	22466			

TYPE K1   OPEN BRAKE FIRST

Built: 1933 – 35. These vintage vehicles are of 'birdcage' design, with a guard's lookout on the roof.
Builder: .
Bogies: Pensylvania.
Accommodation: 50/– 1T.
Heating: Dual.
Computer Numbers: 50 88 81 48 005 – 025.

Length over Buffers: 23.32 m.
Weight: 41.5 tonnes.
Max. Speed: 140 km/h.

28106 | 28107 | 28108 | 28110 | 28112 | 28116 | 28118 |

TYPE K1   OPEN BRAKE FIRST

Built: 1933 – 34.   **Builder:** .
Bogies: Pensylvania.   **Length over Buffers:** 23.32 m.
Accommodation: 39/– 1T.   **Weight:** 43 tonnes.
Heating: Dual.   **Max. Speed:** 140 km/h.
Computer Numbers: 50 88 87 48 001 – 015.

28903 | 28905 | 28907 | 28908 | 28910 | 28913 | 28914 | 28915
28904 | 28906 |

PRE-WAR TYPE L SLAM DOOR STOCK

This stock is presumably museum stock for steam specials.

TYPE L   FIRST

Built: 1933.   **Builder:** .
Bogies: **Length over Buffers:** .
Accommodation: **Weight:** tonnes.
Heating: Steam.   **Max. Speed:** 120 km/h.
Computer Numbers: 50 88 18 26 413-9.

31113 |

TYPE L   SECOND

Built: 1933.   **Builder:** .
Bogies: **Length over Buffers:** .
Accommodation: **Weight:** tonnes.
Heating: Steam.   **Max. Speed:** 120 km/h.
Computer Numbers: 50 88 20 26 435 – 568.

32035 | 32037 | 32076 | 32143 | 32168 |

TYPE L   COMPOSITE

Built: 1933.   **Builder:** .
Bogies: **Length over Buffers:** .
Accommodation: **Weight:** tonnes.
Heating: Steam.   **Max. Speed:** 120 km/h.
Computer Numbers: 50 88 37 26 402 – 6.

33002 | 33006 |

TYPE L   BRAKE FIRST

Built: 1933.   **Builder:** .
Bogies: **Length over Buffers:** .
Accommodation: **Weight:** tonnes.
Heating: Steam.   **Max. Speed:** 120 km/h.
Computer Numbers: 50 88 81 26 405-7.

38005 |

TYPE L   BRAKE SECOND

Built: 1933.   **Builder:** .
Bogies: **Length over Buffers:** .
Accommodation: **Weight:** tonnes.
Heating: Steam.   **Max. Speed:** 120 km/h.
Computer Numbers: 50 88 82 26 425-4.

39025 |

▲ Type K1 'Birdcage' brake first No. 28107 at Sint Niklaas on 5th August 1994.   *Peter Fox*

▼ A rake of M4 stock headed by driving brake open first No. 58038 at the head of the 11.04 Oostende – Kortrijk – Schaarbeek service seen at Brugge on 4th August 1993.   *David Brown*

4XXXX SERIES TYPE M1, M2 & M3 STOCK

TYPE M2   OPEN FIRST

Built: 1958 – 60.
Bogies: Schlieren type 23.
Accommodation: 68/– 1T.
Heating: Dual.
Computer Numbers: 50 88 18 48 (38 e) 601 – 635.

Builder: .
Length over Buffers: 24.00 m.
Weight: 34.5 tonnes.
Max. Speed: 120 km/h.

e Electric heating only.

41001 e	41006	41011	41015	41019	41023	41028	41032
41002	41007	41012 e	41016	41020	41024	41029	41033
41003 e	41008	41013	41017	41021	41025	41030	41034
41004 e	41009	41014	41018	41022	41026	41031 e	41035
41005	41010						

TYPE M1   OPEN SECOND

Built: 1937. Push-pull fitted.
Bogies: Pensylvania.
Accommodation: –/94 1T.
Heating: Steam.
Computer Numbers: 50 88 27 26 602/5/30/43/44/63.

Builder: .
Length over Buffers: 22.76 m.
Weight: 43.9 tonnes.
Max. Speed: 120 km/h.

42014	42062	42094	42097	42128

TYPE M2   OPEN SECOND

Built: 1958 – 60.
Bogies: Schlieren type 23.
Accommodation: –/106 1T.
Heating: Dual.
Computer Numbers: 50 88 20 48 (38 e) 601 – 950.

Builder: .
Length over Buffers: 24.00 m.
Weight: 33.6 tonnes.
Max. Speed: 120 km/h.

e Electric heating only.
p Push-pull fitted.

42301	42329	42357	42386	42414	42442	42471	42500 p
42302	42330	42358	42387	42415	42444	42472	42501
42303 e	42331	42360 e	42388	42416	42445 e	42473	42502 p
42304	42332	42361	42389 e	42417 p	42446 e	42474	42503
42305	42333	42362 e	42390	42418	42447 e	42475	42504
42306	42334	42363 e	42391	42419 e	42448	42476	42505
42307	42335	42364 p	42392 e	42420 p	42449	42477	42506
42308	42336	42365	42393	42421	42450 e	42478	42507
42309 e	42337	42366	42394 p	42422 e	42451	42479	42508
42310	42338	42367	42395	42423 e	42452	42480	42509
42311 p	42339	42368	42396	42424 e	42453	42482 e	42510
42312	42340	42369	42397	42425	42454	42483 e	42511 e
42313	42341	42370 p	42398	42426	42455	42484	42512
42314 e	42342	42371	42399	42427	42456	42485	42513
42315	42343	42372	42400	42428	42457	42486	42514
42316	42344	42373	42401 e	42429	42458	42487	42515
42317	42345	42374 e	42402	42430	42459 p	42488	42516
42318	42346	42375 p	42403 p	42431	42460	42489	42517 e
42319	42347 p	42376	42404	42432	42461	42490	42518
42320 e	42348 p	42377	42405	42433 p	42462 e	42491	42519 p
42321	42349 p	42378 p	42406 e	42434 e	42463	42492	42520 p
42322	42350	42379	42407	42435 e	42464	42493	42521 e
42323	42351	42380	42408	42436	42465	42494 p	42522
42324	42352	42381 e	42409	42437	42466	42495	42523
42325	42353	42382 e	42410	42438	42467	42496 p	42524
42326	42354	42383	42411	42439	42468	42497	42525 p
42327	42355 e	42384	42412	42440	42469	42498	42526 e
42328	42356	42385	42413	42441	42470	42499	42527

42528	42544	42560	42576 p	42591	42606	42621	42636 e
42529	42545	42561	42577 p	42592	42607	42622 p	42637
42530 e	42546	42562	42578	42593 e	42608 e	42623 e	42638 p
42531 p	42547	42563	42579	42594	42609 e	42624	42639
42532	42548	42564 p	42580	42595 e	42610	42625	42640
42533	42549 p	42565 e	42581	42596 e	42611	42626 e	42641 e
42534	42550	42566	42582	42597 e	42612 e	42627	42642 p
42535 e	42551	42567	42583	42598	42613	42628 p	42643
42536 p	42552	42568	42584	42599	42614	42629	42644 p
42537 p	42553	42569	42585	42600	42615	42630	42645 p
42538	42554	42570	42586 p	42601 e	42616	42631 p	42646
42539	42555	42571 p	42587	42602	42617	42632 e	42647 p
42540	42556	42572	42588 p	42603	42618	42633 e	42648
42541	42557	42573 e	42589	42604	42619	42634 e	42649 p
42542 p	42558 p	42574 p	42590 p	42605	42620 p	42635 e	42650 e
42543 e	42559	42575					

TYPE M1   OPEN COMPOSITE

Built: 1937. Push-pull fitted.
Bogies: Pensylvania.
Accommodation: 38/36 1T.
Heating: Steam.
Builder: .
Length over Buffers: 22.76 m.
Weight: 42.2 tonnes.
Max. Speed: 120 km/h.
Computer Numbers: 50 88 38 26 624-7 and 637-9.

43045   43078

TYPE M2   OPEN COMPOSITE

Built: 1958 – 60.
Bogies: Schlieren type 23.
Accommodation: 36/47 1T.
Heating: Dual.
Builder: .
Length over Buffers: 24.00 m.
Weight: 34.4 tonnes.
Max. Speed: 120 km/h.
Computer Numbers: 50 88 39 48 (38 e) 601 – 704.

e Electric heating only.
p Push-pull fitted.

43201 p	43214 p	43227	43240 e	43253	43266	43279	43292
43202 e	43215 p	43228	43241	43254 e	43267 e	43280 e	43293
43203	43216 e	43229 p	43242	43255	43268	43281 p	43294
43204 e	43217 p	43230 p	43243	43256 p	43269	43282 p	43295 p
43205	43218 p	43231	43244 e	43257 e	43270 e	43283	43297 p
43206	43219	43232	43245	43258	43271	43284	43298 p
43207	43220	43233 e	43246	43259	43272 e	43285 p	43299 e
43208	43221	43234 p	43247 e	43260 e	43273	43286 p	43300
43209	43222 p	43235	43248	43261	43274	43287	43301
43210	43223	43236	43249	43262	43275 p	43288	43302
43211	43224	43237	43250	43263 e	43276	43289	43303 p
43212	43225	43238	43251 e	43264	43277	43290 e	43304
43213 p	43226	43239	43252 p	43265	43278	43291 p	

TYPE M1   DRIVING BRAKE OPEN SECOND

Built: 1937. Push-pull driving trailer.
Bogies: Pensylvania.
Accommodation: – /77 1T.
Heating: Steam.
Builder: .
Length over Buffers: 22.76 m.
Weight: 41.9 tonnes.
Max. Speed: 120 km/h.
Computer Number: 50 88 82 26 649-9.

49108

TYPE M2   BRAKE OPEN SECOND

Built: 1958 – 60.
Bogies: Schlieren type 23.
Accommodation: – /75 1T.
Builder: .
Length over Buffers: 24.00 m.
Weight: 32.4 tonnes.

Heating: Dual.　　　　　　　　　　　**Max. Speed:** 120 km/h.
Computer Numbers: 50 88 82 48 (38 e) 601 – 716.

e Electric heating only.
p Converted to push-pull driving trailer.

49201	49216	49231	49246	49260 e	49274 p	49289	49303
49202	49217	49232 p	49247	49261 e	49275	49290	49304
49203	49218 e	49233	49248	49262	49276	49291	49305 p
49204	49219 e	49234 p	49249	49263	49277	49292 p	49306
49205	49220	49235	49250	49264 p	49278	49293 p	49307 p
49206 e	49221	49236 p	49251	49265	49279	49294	49308
49207	49222 e	49237 p	49252 p	49266 p	49281	49295 e	49309
49208	49223	49238	49253 e	49267	49282	49296	49310
49209	49224	49239	49254	49268	49283	49297	49311
49210 p	49225	49240	49255	49269	49284 p	49298 p	49312
49211 p	49226	49241 p	49256 e	49270	49285 p	49299	49313
49212 p	49227	49242	49257	49271 p	49286 p	49300	49314
49213	49228	49243	49258 e	49272	49287	49301	49315
49214	49229	49244	49259	49273	49288	49302	49316 p
49215	49230	49245					

TYPE M2　　　DRIVING BRAKE OPEN SECOND

Built: 1958 – 60. Push-pull driving trailer.　**Builder:** .
Bogies: Schlieren type 23.　　　　　　　**Length over Buffers:** 24.00 m.
Accommodation: – /65 1T.　　　　　　　**Weight:** 32.4 tonnes.
Heating: Dual.　　　　　　　　　　　**Max. Speed:** 120 km/h.
Computer Numbers: 50 88 87 48 (38 e) 601 – 615.

e Electric heating only.

49901 e	49903	49905	49907 e	49909	49911	49913	49915
49902	49904 e	49906	49908	49910 e	49912	49914	

5XXXX SERIES TYPE M4 & M5 STOCK
TYPE M4　　　　　　　　　　OPEN FIRST

Built: 1979 – 80.　　　　　　　　　　**Builder:** BN.
Bogies: Fiat type Y32.　　　　　　　**Length over Buffers:** 24.26 m.
Accommodation: 80/ – 1T.　　　　　　**Weight:** 38 tonnes.
Heating: Electric.　　　　　　　　　**Max. Speed:** 160 km/h.
Computer Numbers: 50 88 19 78 001 – 050.

p Push-pull fitted.

51001	51008	51015	51021	51027	51033	51039 p	51045 p
51002	51009	51016	51022	51028	51034 p	51040 p	51046 p
51003	51010	51017	51023	51029	51035 p	51041 p	51047 p
51004	51011	51018	51024	51030	51036 p	51042 p	51048 p
51005	51012	51019	51025	51031	51037 p	51043 p	51049 p
51006	51013	51020	51026	51032	51038 p	51044 p	51050 p
51007	51014						

TYPE M5　　　DOUBLE-DECK OPEN FIRST

Built: 1988 – 89. Push-pull fitted.　　　**Builder:** .
Bogies: .　　　　　　　　　　　　　**Length over Buffers:** . m.
Accommodation: 142/ – 2T.　　　　　　**Weight:** 44 tonnes.
Heating: Electric.　　　　　　　　　**Max. Speed:** 140 km/h.
Computer Numbers: 50 88 16 38 001 – 015.

51501	51503	51505	51507	51509	51511	51513	51515
51502	51504	51506	51508	51510	51512	51514	

TYPE M4

OPEN SECOND

Built: 1980 – 83.
Bogies: Fiat type Y32.
Accommodation: −/112 1T.
Heating: Electric.
Computer Numbers: 50 88 20 78 001 – 430.

Builder: .
Length over Buffers: 24.26 m.
Weight: 39 tonnes.
Max. Speed: 160 km/h.

p Push-pull fitted.

52001	52055	52109	52164	52218	52272 p	52325 p	52378 p
52002	52056	52110	52165	52219	52273 p	52326 p	52379 p
52003	52057	52111	52166	52220	52274 p	52327 p	52380 p
52004	52058	52112	52167	52221	52275 p	52328 p	52381 p
52005	52059	52113	52168	52222	52276 p	52329 p	52382 p
52006	52060	52114	52169	52223	52277 p	52330 p	52383 p
52007	52061	52115	52170	52224	52278 p	52331 p	52384 p
52008	52062	52116	52171	52225	52279 p	52332 p	52385 p
52009	52063	52117	52172	52226	52280 p	52333 p	52386 p
52010	52064	52118	52173	52227	52281 p	52334 p	52387 p
52011	52065	52119	52174	52228	52282 p	52335 p	52388 p
52012	52066	52120	52175	52229	52283 p	52336 p	52389 p
52013	52067	52121	52176	52230	52284 p	52337 p	52390 p
52014	52068	52122	52177	52231	52285 p	52338 p	52391 p
52015	52069	52123	52178	52232	52286 p	52339 p	52392 p
52016	52070	52124	52179	52233	52287 p	52340 p	52393 p
52017	52071	52125	52180	52234	52288 p	52341 p	52394 p
52018	52072	52126	52181	52235	52289 p	52342 p	52395 p
52019	52073	52127	52182	52236	52290 p	52343 p	52396 p
52020	52074	52128	52183	52237	52291 p	52344 p	52397 p
52021	52075	52129	52184	52238	52292 p	52345 p	52398 p
52022	52076	52130	52185	52239	52293 p	52346 p	52399 p
52023	52077	52131	52186	52240	52294 p	52347 p	52400 p
52024	52078	52132	52187	52241	52295 p	52348 p	52401 p
52025	52079	52133	52188	52242	52296 p	52349 p	52402 p
52026	52080	52134	52189	52243	52297 p	52350 p	52403 p
52027	52081	52135	52190	52244	52298 p	52351 p	52404 p
52028	52082	52136	52191	52245	52299 p	52352 p	52405 p
52029	52083	52137	52192	52246	52300 p	52353 p	52406 p
52030	52084	52138	52193	52247	52301 p	52354 p	52407 p
52031	52085	52139	52194	52248 p	52302 p	52355 p	52408 p
52032	52086	52140	52195	52249 p	52303 p	52356 p	52409 p
52033	52087	52141	52196	52250 p	52304 p	52357 p	52410 p
52034	52088	52142	52197	52251 p	52305 p	52358 p	52411 p
52035	52089	52143	52198	52252 p	52306 p	52359 p	52412 p
52036	52090	52144	52199	52253 p	52307 p	52360 p	52413 p
52037	52091	52145	52200	52254 p	52308 p	52361 p	52414 p
52038	52092	52146	52201	52255 p	52309 p	52362 p	52415 p
52039	52093	52147	52202	52256 p	52310 p	52363 p	52416 p
52040	52094	52148	52203	52257 p	52311 p	52364 p	52417 p
52041	52095	52149	52204	52258 p	52312 p	52365 p	52418 p
52042	52096	52150	52205	52259 p	52313 p	52366 p	52419 p
52043	52097	52152	52206	52260 p	52314 p	52367 p	52420 p
52044	52098	52153	52207	52261 p	52315 p	52368 p	52421 p
52045	52099	52154	52208	52262 p	52316 p	52369 p	52422 p
52046	52100	52155	52209	52263 p	52317 p	52370 p	52423 p
52047	52101	52156	52210	52264 p	52318 p	52371 p	52424 p
52048	52102	52157	52211	52265 p	52319 p	52372 p	52425 p
52049	52103	52158	52212	52266 p	52320 p	52373 p	52426 p
52050	52104	52159	52213	52267 p	52321 p	52374 p	52427 p
52051	52105	52160	52214	52268 p	52322 p	52375 p	52428 p
52052	52106	52161	52215	52269 p	52323 p	52376 p	52429 p
52053	52107	52162	52216	52270 p	52324 p	52377 p	52430 p
52054	52108	52163	52217	52271 p			

TYPE M5   DOUBLE-DECK OPEN SECOND

Built: 1988 – 89. Push-pull fitted.
Bogies: .
Accommodation: – /146 2T.
Heating: Electric.
Computer Numbers: 50 88 26 38 001 – 097.

Builder: .
Length over Buffers: . m.
Weight: 43.8 tonnes.
Max. Speed: 140 km/h.

52501	52514	52526	52538	52550	52562	52574	52586
52502	52515	52527	52539	52551	52563	52575	52587
52503	52516	52528	52540	52552	52564	52576	52588
52504	52517	52529	52541	52553	52565	52577	52589
52505	52518	52530	52542	52554	52566	52578	52590
52506	52519	52531	52543	52555	52567	52579	52591
52507	52520	52532	52544	52556	52568	52580	52592
52508	52521	52533	52545	52557	52569	52581	52593
52509	52522	52534	52546	52558	52570	52582	52594
52510	52523	52535	52547	52559	52571	52583	52595
52511	52524	52536	52548	52560	52572	52584	52596
52512	52525	52537	52549	52561	52573	52585	52597
52513							

TYPE M4   BRAKE OPEN FIRST

Built: 1982.
Bogies: Fiat type Y32.
Accommodation: 56/– 1T.
Heating: Electric.
Computer Numbers: 50 88 81 78 001 – 033.

Builder: BN .
Length over Buffers: 24.26 m.
Weight: 37.2 tonnes.
Max. Speed: 160 km/h.

58001	58006	58010	58014	58018	58022	58026	58030
58002	58007	58011	58015	58019	58023	58027	58031
58003	58008	58012	58016	58020	58024	58028	58032
58004	58009	58013	58017	58021	58025	58029	58033
58005							

TYPE M4   DRIVING BRAKE OPEN FIRST

Built: 1983. Push-pull driving trailer.
Bogies: Fiat type Y32.
Accommodation: 48/– 1T.
Heating: Electric.
Computer Numbers: 50 88 81 78 034 – 065.

Builder: BN.
Length over Buffers: 24.26 m.
Weight: 39 tonnes.
Max. Speed: 160 km/h.

58034	58038	58042	58046	58050	58054	58058	58062
58035	58039	58043	58047	58051	58055	58059	58063
58036	58040	58044	58048	58052	58056	58060	58064
58037	58041	58045	58049	58053	58057	58061	58065

TYPE M4   BRAKE OPEN SECOND

Built: 1983 – 84.
Bogies: Fiat type Y32.
Accommodation: – /64 1T.
Heating: Electric.
Computer Numbers: 50 88 82 78 001 – 035.
Computer Numbers: 50 88 87 78 006 – 023 (k).

Builder: .
Length over Buffers: 24.26 m.
Weight: 39.5 tonnes.
Max. Speed: 160 km/h.

k With buffet service.
p Converted to push-pull driving trailer.

59901	59906 k	59911 k	59916	59920	59924	59928 p	59932 p
59902	59907 k	59912 k	59917	59921	59925	59929 p	59933 p
59903	59908	59913	59918 k	59922 k	59926 p	59930 p	59934 p
59904	59909 k	59914 k	59919 k	59923 k	59927 p	59931 p	59935 p
59905	59910	59915 k					

TYPE M5 DOUBLE-DECK DRIVING OPEN SECOND

Built: 1988 – 89. Push-pull driving trailer.
Bogies: .
Accommodation: – /118 2T.
Heating: Electric.
Computer Numbers: 50 88 82 38 001 – 018.

Builder: .
Length over Buffers: . m.
Weight: 49.3 tonnes.
Max. Speed: 140 km/h.

59951	59954	59957	59959	59961	59963	59965	59967
59952	59955	59958	59960	59962	59964	59966	59968
59953	59956						

POSTAL VANS WITH GENERATORS

Built: 1933 – 34.
Bogies: Pensylvania.
Weight: 46 tonnes.
Max. Speed: 120 km/h.
Computer Numbers: 50 88 92 66 907/8/911.

Length over Buffers: 15.60 m.
Heating: Steam (Dual*).

77019 | 77020 | 77023 |

MISCELLANEOUS DEPARTMENTAL STOCK

11	60 88 99 70 011-6	Traction department test coach
13	60 88 99 70 013-2	Traction department test coach
31	60 88 80 69 031-8	Medical coach
32	60 88 99 69 032-6	Medical coach
41	60 88 99 10 041-6	Cinema coach
51	60 88 99 69 051-5	Emergency vehicle
52	60 88 99 69 052-3	Emergency vehicle
53	60 88 99 69 053-1	Emergency vehicle
54	60 88 99 69 054-9	Emergency vehicle
55	60 88 99 69 055-6	Emergency vehicle
61	60 88 99 69 101-9	Signalling school coach
62	60 88 99 69 102-7	Signalling school coach
63	60 88 99 69 103-5	Signalling school coach
64	60 88 99 69 104-3	Signalling school coach
65	60 88 99 69 105-0	Signalling school coach
71	60 88 99 09 001-3	Infrastructure dept. coach
72	60 88 99 09 002-1	Infrastructure dept. coach
201	60 88 99 29 201-5	Infrastructure dept. coach
202	60 88 99 29 202-3	Infrastructure dept. coach
203	60 88 99 29 203-1	Infrastructure dept. coach
204	60 88 99 29 204-9	Infrastructure dept. coach
205	60 88 99 29 205-6	Infrastructure dept. coach
206	60 88 99 29 206-4	Infrastructure dept. coach
207	60 88 99 29 207-2	Infrastructure dept. coach
208	60 88 99 29 208-0	Infrastructure dept. coach
209	60 88 99 29 209-8	Infrastructure dept. coach
210	60 88 99 29 210-6	Infrastructure dept. coach
211	60 88 99 29 211-4	Infrastructure dept. coach
212	60 88 99 29 212-2	Infrastructure dept. coach
213	60 88 99 29 213-0	Infrastructure dept. coach
214	60 88 99 29 214-8	Infrastructure dept. coach
215	60 88 99 29 215-5	Infrastructure dept. coach
216	60 88 99 29 216-3	Infrastructure dept. coach
217	60 88 99 29 217-1	Infrastructure dept. coach
218	60 88 99 29 218-9	Infrastructure dept. coach
223	60 88 99 48 223-6	Infrastructure dept. coach
224	60 88 99 29 224-7	Infrastructure dept. coach
225	60 88 99 29 225-4	Infrastructure dept. coach
226	60 88 99 29 226-2	Infrastructure dept. coach
601	60 88 99 80 001-5	Infrastructure dept. test coach
602	60 88 99 89 002-4	Infrastructure dept. test coach
820	60 88 99 39 020-7	Exhibition coach

BELGIAN PRESERVED LOCOMOTIVES & RAILCARS
STATUS CODES

A   Active (location could vary).
P   Plinthed
K   Retained for special excursions.

M   Museum or Museum line loco.
R   Under restoration (perhaps at another place).
S   Stored or for spares.

STEAM LOCOMOTIVES:

Number	Wheels	Built	Status	Location
1.002	4 – 6 – 2	1921	MR	FLV
7.039	4 – 6 – 0	1921	MS	FLV
10.018	4 – 6 – 2	1911	MS	FLV
12.004	4 – 4 – 2	1939	MA	FLV
16.042	4 – 4 – 2T	1909	MS	FLV
18.051	4 – 4 – 0	1905	MS	FLV
29.013	2 – 8 – 0	1945	MA	FLV
41.195	0 – 6 – 0	1910	P	FC
44.021	0 – 6 – 0	1906	MS	FLV
44.225	0 – 6 – 0	1907	MS	FLV
53.320	0 – 8 – 0T	1906	MS	FLV
64.045	4 – 6 – 0	1918	MS	FLV
2	2 – 2 – 2ST	1842	M	Brussels Nord
615	0 – 8 – 0T	1859	MS	FLV
1151	0 – 6 – 0PT	1879	MS	FLV
3364	0 – 4 – 0VB	1877	MP	Steamtown USA

DIESEL & ELECTRIC LOCOMOTIVES:

Number	Wheels	Built	Status	Location
2912	Bo – Bo e	1949	MS	FLV
2913	Bo – Bo e	1949	P	CWFM
5204	Co – Co de	1955	MS	FAZ. Stored for PFT.
5910	Bo – Bo de	1955	MA	FNDM. Restored as 210.010
5922	Bo – Bo de	1955	MA	Raeren. Vennbahn.
5927	Bo – Bo de	1955	MS	FAZ. Stored for PFT.
5930	Bo – Bo de	1955	MA	Raeren. Vennbahn.
6041	Bo – Bo de	1965	MA	NK.
6077	Bo – Bo de	1965	MA	FSR for PFT.
6106	Bo – Bo de	1965	MA	FSR for PFT.
6406	BB dh	1962	MS	FLV
7103	D dh	1957	MS	FLV
7209	D dh	1956	MS	FNDM

DIESEL & ELECTRIC RAILCARS:

Number	Wheels	Built	Status	Location
4001	3-car DHMU	1957	MA	CFV3V
4006	3-car DHMU	1957	MS	LK
4302	2 – B DHMU	1954	MA	SDP Baasrode
4333	2 – B DHMU	1955	MA	FSR. PFT
4602	1A – A1 DHMU	1952	MA	FSR. PFT
4604	1A – A1 DHMU	1952	P	ULM Isières
4605	1A – A1 DHMU	1952	MS	FSR. PFT
4610	1A – A1 DHMU	1952	MS	Maubeuge, France
4611	1A – A1 DHMU	1952	MA	CFV3V Mariembourg
4614	1A – A1 DHMU	1952	MA	
4616	1A – A1 DHMU	1952	MA	CFV3V Mariembourg
4618	1A – A1 DHMU	1952	MA	FSR. PFT as 554.18
4620	1A – A1 DHMU	1952	MA	SCM Maldegem
4903	1A – A1 DMMU	1942	MS	FLV

Number	Wheels	Built	Status	Location
4905	1A – A1 DMMU	1942	MR	FNDM
4906	1A – A1 DMMU	1942	MA	FSR. PFT as 553.29
551.48	B DMMU	1939	MS	FTY
608.05	1A – A1 DMMU	1939	MS	CWFM
654.02	1/3 DEMU	1936	MS	FLV
ES 308	A – A DMMU	1939	MA	FSR. PFT as 551.26
002	2-car EMU	1939	MS	FLV
002	2-car EMU	1935	MS	GT
502	2-car EMU	1955	MR	FSR. PFT
901	2-car EMU	1957	MR	CWFM
7.312/ 7.724	4-car EMU	1935	MA	FSR

PRINCIPAL FOREIGN LOCOS ETC PRESERVED IN BELGIUM:

Number	Wheels	Built	Status	Location
'26.101'	2 – 10 – 0	1943	MA	FSR. PFT ex Ty2.3554 Poland.
50.3666	2 – 10 – 0	1943	MA	Raeren. Vennbahn. ex DR.
50.3696	2 – 10 – 0	1939	MA	CFV3V. ex DR.
52.3314	2 – 10 – 0	1944	MR	GT. CFV3V ex ÖBB.
52.8200	2 – 10 – 0	1943	MR	GT. CFV3V ex DR.
64.250	2 – 6 – 2T	1930	MR	GT. CFV3V ex DB.
798 662	A1 DMMU	1955	MA	CFV3V as 551.662. ex DB.
798 669	A1 DMMU	1955	MA	CFV3V as 551.669. ex DB.
228 792	CC DH	1969	MA	Raeren. Vennbahn. ex DR.
X 3898	B – 2 DMMU	1957	MA	CFV3V ex SNCF.
X 3998	B – 2 DMMU	1957	MA	CFV3V ex SNCF.
Y 2498	B DM	1968	MA	CFV3V ex SNCF.
Y 6563	B DE	1957	MA	CFV3V ex SNCF.

For society and railway abbreviations see the "Museums and Museum Lines" section.

Class 1100 No. 1149 at Rotterdam CS on 11th January 1994.   Dr A.T. Sumner

2. NETHERLANDS RAILWAYS (NS)

The Dutch name for the Netherlands Railways is Nederlandse Spoorwegen, hereafter abreviated to NS. The NS is a relatively small system and approximately two thirds of all routes are electrified at 1500 V d.c. with overhead wire collection. Comprehensive maps of the system are to be found on the next four pages. Language presents no problem, since most Dutch people speak good English, but restaurant menus are often in dutch only, so a dictionary or phrase book can still be useful. Different numbering series were used for locos and multiple units, but with renumbering and condemnations, numbers do not now duplicate.

DEPOTS & WORKSHOPS

Not all NS locos and units have depot allocations. The vast majority are common-user but there are some definite allocations, as all the electric locos are allocated to Maastricht whilst certain 2200s are definitely allocated to Feijenoord and the 6400s are at Zwolle. The situation can be summarised as follows:

Electric locos	Maastricht
Diesel locos	Feijenoord, Watergraafsmeer, Zwolle
EMUs	Amsterdam Zaanstraat, Leidschendamm, Maastricht, Onnen
DMUs	Maastricht, Zwolle, Onnen

The main workshops are at Haarlem (for all units) and Tilburg (for all locos and the power units of DMUs.

There are many places where EMUs stable, but the main locations where units and some locos will be found are: Alkmaar, Amersfoort, Arnhem, Botlek*, Den Haag CS, Eindhoven, Goes, Groningen, Heerlen, Hengelo, Kijfhoek Yard*, Leeuwarden, Nijmegen, Roosendaal, Rotterdan CS, Sittard, Utrecht, Venlo, Vlissingen, Waalhaven Zuid* and Zutphen. (* − locos only).

PASSENGER TRAINS

The NS timetable is almost entirely regular interval with most routes having half-hourly services and many routes four trains per hour.

There are now three types of train category on the NS. Intercity, stoptreinen and sneltreinen. Stoptreinen are stopping trains and are generally either EMUs or push-pull double-decker sets. Intercity trains are generally either Koploper EMUs or are loco-hauled. Principal internal loco-hauled routes (including workings into adjacent countries are:

Table 10. Amsterdam − Den Haag − Rotterdam − Dordrecht − Roosendaal − Brussels. These are push-pull trains with SNCB dual-voltage class 11 electric locos and plan ICR3 stock. Trains which go through to France are generally SNCB class 25.5 hauled.

Table 20. Zandvoort − Haarlem − Amsterdam − Utrecht − 's Hertogenbosch − Eindhoven − Sittard − Maastricht/Heerlen. These trains are loco hauled with either class 1200 or 1600, but 1300s are also used. Because loads are heavy, the ICR coaches are strengthened with plan W stock and 1100s are rare. In summer the Maastricht services convey a bicycle brake.

Table 40. Amsterdam − Rotterdam − Utrecht − Arnhem/Nijmegen − Köln/Hagen. Amsterdam − Köln/Hagen services are worked by 1100, 1300 and 1600 electrics with some 1200 turns. The Köln/Hagen services are worked forward from Emmerich by DB class 110 electrics. The Köln via Nijmegen services are worked forward from Arnhem with DB 215, 216 or 218 series diesel hydraulics.

Table 50. Den Haag − Rotterdam − Dordrecht − Tilburg − Eindhoven − Venlo − (Köln). Den Haag − Venlo/Köln services are loco-hauled mainly with class 1600s, although other classes also appear. Köln services are usually worked forward from Venlo by DB 110 series electrics.

Other services. There are other odd loco-hauled services which can be found, e.g. the 15.40 Zwolle − Maastricht. The NS timetable says that all non-double-decker loco-hauled services have telephones, and puts a telephone symbol at the top of the column. This is therefore a good way of picking out the hauled services (but not much use if you want to use a phone, since the phones had not been fitted at the time of writing except in a few Benelux push-pull firsts. All long distance international trains are loco-hauled generally with 1600s.

'Sneltrein' is a new category which fits in between Intercity and 'Stoptrein'. These are generally are Koploper or Hondekop EMUs or push-pull 1600 double-deckers.

Nederlandse Spoorwegen

NS NETWORK MAPS

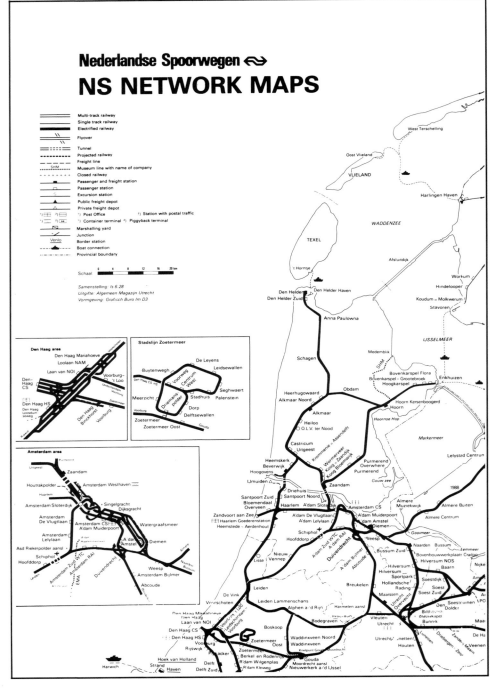

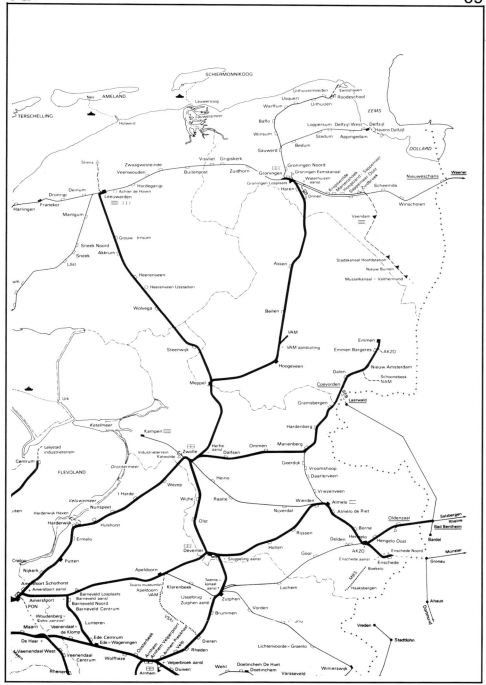

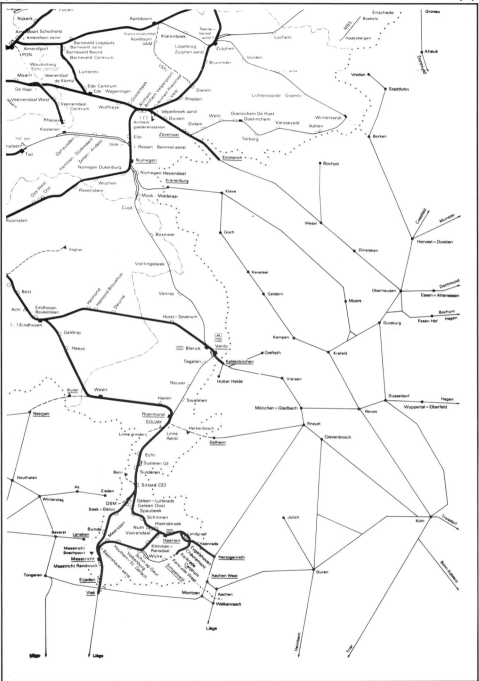

DIESEL SHUNTING LOCOMOTIVES
CLASS 200   B

These small locomotives known as "Siks" (goats) are to be found on light duties in freight yards and engineers locations throughout the NS system. The light overall weight and robust construction have contributed to the longevity of the class. Formerly painted dark green with cast number plates.

Built: 1934 – 51.
Builder: Werkspoor (281 – 06 built by NS Zwolle Works).
Engine: Stork R153 of 63 kW.
Transmission: Electric. Two Heemaf TM6 or Smit GT 322/7 axle-hung.
Train Heating: None.   **Weight in Full Working Order:** 21 (23 c) tonnes.
Maximum Tractive Effort: 39 kN.   **Length over Buffers:** 7.22 m.
Driving Wheel Dia.: 1000 mm.   **Max. Speed:** 60 km/h.

c Fitted with telescopic crane.

203	228	249	271	297	315	332	349
204	229	250 c	274 c	298	316	334	350
209	230	252 c	276 c	299	318	335	351
210	231	253	278	300	319	336	352
211	232	254	279	301	320	337	353
213	234	255	281	302	321	338	355 c
214	235	256	283	303	322	339	357
215	238	257	284 c	305	323	340	358
217	241	259	285	306	324	341	359
218	242 c	260	286	307	325	342	360 c
219	243	262	288	308	326	343	361 c
222	244	263	289	309 c	327	344	362 c
223	245	264	290	310	328	345	363
225	246 c	265 c	291	312	329	346	368 c
226	247	267	292	313	330	347	369
227 c	248 c	270	296	314	331	348	

CLASS 600   C

Instantly recognisable to the British eye, based on the BR Class 08, these locomotives perform similar duties.

Built: 1950 – 57.
Builder: English Electric (Dick Kerr Works, Preston).
Engine: English Electric 6KT of 294 kW.
Transmission: Electric. Two EE 506 axle-hung traction motors.
Train Heating: None.   **Weight in Full Working Order:** 47 tonnes.
Maximum Tractive Effort: 143 kN.   **Length over Buffers:** 9.07 m.
Driving Wheel Dia.: 1230 mm.   **Max. Speed:** 30 km/h.

603	618	628	636 (S)	641	647	655	661
604	619	629	637 (S)	643 (S)	648	656	662
608	622	631	638 (S)	644	650	657	663
610	623	633 (S)	639 (S)	645	651	658	664
617	624	635 (S)	640 (S)	646 (S)	653	660	665

Fitted with Radio Remote Control & Renumbered.

671 (601)	677 (612)	683 (621)	689 (652)
672 (602)	678 (613)	684 (626)	690 (654)
673 (605)	679 (614)	685 (627)	691 (642)
674 (606)	680 (615)	686 (630)	692 (649)
675 (607)	681 (616)	687 (632)	693 (659)
676 (611)	682 (620)	688 (634)	

ELECTRIC LOCOMOTIVES
CLASS 1100 Bo – Bo

These locomotives are based on the SNCF Class BB 8100 dating from 1949, modified with spring-borne traction motors. Alterations by the NS have included the fitting of roller bearings and larger sleeve-type buffers as carried by Class 1600. From 1978 new nose-ends were fitted. 1101 – 50 were originally liveried in light blue, but this gave way in 1954 to dark blue with polished raised metal bands. Since 1971, the current NS grey and yellow livery has been applied to all locos. The locos work mixed-traffic duties all over the NS, but are gradually being withdrawn.

Built: 1950 – 56. (Rebuilt by NS 1978 – 82).
Builder-Mech. Parts: Alsthom.
Builder-Elec. Parts: Alsthom.
Traction Motors: 4 x Alsthom TA628A frame-mounted.
One Hour Rating: 2030 kW.   **Weight:** 83 tonnes.
Maximum Tractive Effort: 152 kN.   **Length over Buffers:** 14.110 m.
Driving Wheel Dia.: 1250 mm.   **Max. Speed:** 135 km/h.

1101		1108		1113	1119		1130	(S)	1142	1149		1155	(S)
1102	(S)	1109	(S)	1114	1122		1132		1144	1151	(S)	1157	(S)
1103	(S)	1110		1115	1123	(S)	1134		1145	1152		1158	(S)
1104	(S)	1111		1116	1124		1135	(S)	1147	1153	(S)	1159	
1106	(S)	1112	(S)	1117	1127		1136		1148	1154	(S)	1160	
1107													

CLASS 1200 Co – Co

The striking 1200s, originally built for freight haulage were constructed as 'kit-form' locomotives with the bogies being supplied by Baldwin and electrical components by Westinghouse, the clasic American styling clearly showing their design origin. Until refurbishment by the NS, the mixed parentage was displayed on elaborate worksplates carried on the nose ends. These locos, extremely popular with their NS crews, originally carried the light blue (1215 mahogany!) and dark blue liveries but all are now in the standard colours of grey and yellow. Their main passenger duty is on the Intercity service between Zandvoort-aan-Zee and Maastricht/Heerlen. Withdrawals have now commenced.

Built: 1951 – 53.
Builder-Mech. Parts: Werkspoor.
Builder-Elec. Parts: Heemaf.
Traction Motors: 4 x Heemaf TM94 axle-hung.
One Hour Rating: 2360 kW.   **Weight:** 108 tonnes.
Maximum Tractive Effort: 194 kN.   **Length over Buffers:** 18.085 m.
Driving Wheel Dia.: 1100 mm.   **Max. Speed:** 135 km/h.

1201	1204	1207	1210	1214	1217	1220	(S)	1224
1202	1205	1208	1211	1215	1218	1221		1225
1203	1206	1209	1213	1216	1219	1222	(S)	

CLASS 1300 Co – Co

The impressive-looking Class 1300 are based on the SNCF Class CC 7100 which includes in it's ranks CC 7107, the co-world speed record holder (331 km/h attained in 1955). The NS 1300 duties are much less glamorous, being generally utilised for heavy freight work with limited passenger diagrams. The class has undergone a major refurbishment programme, the external appearance being more in keeping with the Class 1600 livery but with an extremely large NS logo on the body side and an EMU-style lamp assembly on the front end.

Built: 1952 – 56.
Builder-Mech. Parts: Alsthom.
Builder-Elec. Parts: Alsthom.
Traction Motors: 6 x Alsthom TA 628A frame mounted.
One Hour Rating: 3045 kW.   **Weight:** 111 tonnes.
Maximum Tractive Effort: 226 kN.   **Length over Buffers:** 18.952 m.
Driving Wheel Dia.: 1250 mm.   **Max. Speed:** 135 km/h.

1301	DIEREN		1310	BUSSUM
1302	WOERDEN		1311	BEST
1304	CULEMBOURG		1312	ZOETERMEER
1305	ALPHEN AAN DER RIJN		1313	UITGEEST
1306	BRUMMEN		1314	HOORN
1307	ETTEN LEUR		1315	TIEL
1308	NUNSPEET		1316	GELDERMALSEN
1309	SUSTEREN			

CLASS 1600   B – B

These locomotives are based on the SNCF Class BB 7200 designed for a maximum speed of 200 km/h (limited at present to 160 km/h). The locos work mixed traffic duties over all principal routes.

Built: 1981 – 83.
Builder-Mech. Parts: Alsthom.
Builder-Elec. Parts: Alsthom.
Traction Motors: 2 x Alsthom TAB 674 C4 frame mounted.
One Hour Rating: 4400 kW.   **Weight:** 83 tonnes.
Maximum Tractive Effort: 294 kN.   **Length over Buffers:** 17.48 m.
Driving Wheel Dia.: 1250 mm.   **Max. Speed:** 160 km/h.

All push-pull fitted.

1601	AMSTERDAM		1630	ZWOLLE
1602	Schipol		1631	VOORBURG
1603	ZUTPHEN		1632	NIJMEGEN
1604	DORDRECHT		1633	BERGEN OP ZOOM
1605	BREDA		1634	LELYSTAD
1606	HARDERWIJK		1635	ENSCHEDE
1607	VLISSINGEN		1636	HEEREVEEN
1608	'S HERTOGENBOSCH		1637	AMERSFOORT
1609	HOOFDDORP		1638	GRONINGEN
1610	HENGELO		1639	LEIDEN
1611	VENLO		1640	STEENWIJK
1612	GOES		1641	ALMERE
1613	ROERMOND		1642	WEERT
1614	SCHIEDAM		1643	HEERLEN
1615	ZANDVOORT		1644	ROOSENDAAL
1616	OLDENZAAL		1645	MIDDELBURG
1617	ASSEN		1646	LEEUWARDEN
1618	ALMELO		1647	DELFT
1619	MAASTRICHT		1648	VALKENBURG
1620	ARNHEM		1649	OSS
1621	DEVENTER		1650	DEN HAAG
1622	HAARLEM		1651	TILBURG
1623	HILVERSUM		1652	UTRECHT
1624	ALKMAAR		1653	DEN HELDER
1625	SITTARD		1654	GELEEN
1626	MEPPEL		1655	EINDHOVEN
1627	GOUDA		1656	HOOGEVEEN
1628	APELDOORN		1657	ROTTERDAM
1629	EDE		1658	ZAANDAM

CLASS 1700   B – B

This class is virtually identical to the Class 1600, the main difference being the fact that they have auto-couplers. The locos are used in fixed formation sets with the new double-decker DD-AR stock.

Built: 1990 – 94.
Builder-Mech. Parts: Alsthom.
Builder-Elec. Parts: Alsthom.
Traction Motors: 2 x Alsthom TAB 674 C4 frame mounted.

One Hour Rating: 4400 kW.   **Weight:** 83 tonnes.
Maximum Tractive Effort: 294 kN.   **Length over Buffers:** 17.48 m.
Driving Wheel Dia.: 1250 mm.   **Max. Speed:** 160 km/h.

All push-pull fitted.

1701		1742	
1702		1743	WESTSTELLINGWERF
1703		1744	
1704		1745	
1705	DALFSEN	1746	BREDA
1706		1747	
1707		1748	
1708		1749	
1709		1750	
1710		1751	
1711	EMMEN	1752	
1712		1753	
1713		1754	DIEMEN
1714	VEENENDAL	1755	
1715		1756	
1716		1757	
1717		1758	
1718		1759	
1719		1760	
1720	BEILEN	1761	
1721		1762	
1722		1763	
1723		1764	
1724		1765	
1725		1766	
1726		1767	
1727		1768	
1728		1769	
1729		1770	
1730		1771	
1731		1772	
1732		1773	
1733		1774	
1734		1775	
1735	SOEST	1776	
1736	GILZE-RIJEN	1777	
1737		1778	
1738	DUIVENDRECHT	1779	
1739	DALEN	1780	
1740		1781	
1741	PUTTEN		

MAIN-LINE DIESEL LOCOMOTIVES
CLASS 2200   Bo – Bo

These locos which have a cab at one end can be found either double-heading or singly on freight work. The class will shortly be withdrawn when all the new 6400 class have been successfully commissioned.

Built: 1955 – 58.
Builder: Allen (2201 – 2300), Schneider (2301 – 2350).
Engine: Stork Schneider Superior 40C-Lx-8 of 670 kW at 1100 rpm.
Transmission: Electric. 4 Heemaf TM98 traction motors.
Train Heating: None.   **Weight in Full Working Order:** 72 tonnes.
Maximum Tractive Effort: 181 kN.   **Length over Buffers:** 14.100 m.
Driving Wheel Dia.: 950 mm.   **Max. Speed:** 100 km/h.

2201	2204	2210	2215	2270	2308	2328	2363
2202	2207	2211	2260	2278	2323	2336	2377
2203	2209	2212	2264				

Fitted with Radio Remote Control & Renumbered.

2351 (2267)	2365 (2291)	2372 (2307)	2378 (2339)
2352 (2268)	2366 (2294)	2373 (2317)	2379 (2343)
2353 (2303)	2367 (2295)	2374 (2324)	2380 (2344)
2354 (2304)	2368 (2296)	2375 (2332)	2381 (2346)
2361 (2230)	2369 (2297)	2376 (2335)	2382 (2348)
2363 (2252)	2370 (2298)	2377 (2338)	2384 (2342)
2364 (2290)	2371 (2300)		

CLASS 6400   Bo – Bo

New thyristor-controlled locomotives for freight and shunting use.

Built: 1988 – 94.
Builder: MaK.
Engine: MaK of 1180 kW.
Transmission: 4 x three phase BBC traction motors.
Train Heating: None.   **Weight in Full Working Order:** 80 tonnes.
Maximum Tractive Effort: 290 kN.   **Length over Buffers:** 14.40 m.
Driving Wheel Dia.: 1000 mm.   **Max. Speed:** 120 km/h.

6401	Mijndert	6425	Chris
6402	Marinus	6426	Niko
6403	Gijs	6427	Hans
6404	Jo	6428	Dirk
6405	Jan	6429	Hans
6406	Tonnie	6430	Jan Adrianus
6407	Henk	6431	Antonius
6408	Gerard	6432	Hendrikus
6409	Herman	6433	Han
6410	Toon	6434	Henk
6411	Oliver	6435	Joop
6412	Hans	6436	
6413	Foeke	6437	Arie
6414	Sander	6438	
6415	Rens	6439	Geert
6416	Arie	6440	
6417	Bob	6441	Joyce
6418	John	6442	
6419	Willem	6443	
6420	Horst	6444	Eeltje
6421	Sebe	6445	Wijbo
6422	Wim	6446	Jo
6423	Chris	6447	Maurits
6424	Dirk	6448	Rein

6449		John	6485		
6450		Hanja	6486		
6451			6487		
6452		Rein	6488		
6453		Frans	6489		
6454		Wim	6490		
6455		Klaas-Abel	6491		
6456			6492		
6457			6493		Joke
6458		Harry	6494		
6459		Anton	6495		
6460		Leo	6496		
6461	e		6497		
6462	e	Olga	6498		
6463	e	Theo	6499		
6464	e	Jan	6500		
6465	e	Lammert	6501		
6466	e		6502		
6467	e		6503		
6468	e		6504		
6469	e		6505		
6470	e		6506		
6471	e		6507		
6472	e		6508		
6473	e		6509		
6474	e		6510		
6475	e		6511	R	
6476			6512	R	
6477			6513	R	
6478			6514	R	
6479			6515	R	
6480			6516	R	
6481		Lies	6517	R	
6482			6518	R	
6483			6519	R	
6484			6520	R	

DIESEL MULTIPLE UNITS
CLASS DEIII (PLAN U)   3-CAR UNITS

In many respects similar to the 1962 stock EMUs, these three-car EMUs work over the following lines: Dordrecht – Geldermalsen, Roermond – Nijmegen, Zwolle – Enschede/Emmen, and Arnhem – Winterswijk. Automatic doors. PA. Originally painted red, they were known as 'red devils'.

mBDk + B + ABk (DMBSO – TSO – DTCso).

Built: 1960 – 63.
Builder: Werkspoor.
Wheel Arrangement: Bo – Bo + 2 – 2 + 2 – 2.
Engine: SACM MGO-12-BSHR of 735 kW.
Transmission: Electric. Smit GT 38/224 or Metropolitan Vickers MV 139.
Accommodation: 40/88 2T + 24/40 2T.
Weight: 66 + 35 + 35 tonnes.
Length over couplings: 25.17 + 24.09 + 25.17 m.
Max. Speed: 125 km/h.

111	117	122	127	132	137	142	148
112	118	123	128	133	138	144	149
113	119	124	129	134	139	145	150
114	120	125	130	135	140	146	151
115	121	126	131	136	141	147	152
116							

CLASS DEII (PLAN X-v)   2-CAR UNITS

These articulated units (ex 61 – 106 series) were originally liveried in light blue with wings on the front and were nicknamed "blue angels". They have been extensively rebuilt and modernised and have large pods on the roof for pressure ventilation equipment. Duties include Zwolle – Kampen, Arnhem – Nijmegen – Teil, Apeldoorn – Winterswijk and Maastricht – Arnhem – Tiel.

mABk + mBk (DMCO – DMSO).

Built: 1953 – 54. Rebuilt 1975/77 – 82.
Builder: Allan. Rebuilt NS Haarlem.
Wheel Arrangement: Bo – 2 – Bo.
Engine: Cummins NT895R2 of 180 kW (one per car).
Transmission: Electric.
Accommodation: 16/56 1T + –/76 1T.
Length over couplings: 22.70 + 22.70 m.
Weight: 45 + 45 tonnes.
Max. Speed: 120 km/h.

162 (92)	167 (61)	171 (98/100)	175 (68/64)	179 (72/73)	183 (67)
163 (83)	168 (91)	172 (66/86)	176 (64/62)	180 (73/66)	184 (63/65)
164 (106/69)	169 (94)	173 (100/70)	177 (62/82)	181 (99)	185 (102)
165 (103)	170 (69/98)	174 (70/68)	178 (82/72)	182 (75)	186 (77/87)
166 (97)					

3100/3200 CLASSES:

These units represented a change in policy for the NS. The power equipment was based on that used to modernise the DEII units, i.e. a Cummins engine, but Voith hydraulic transmission was used. A new body style was adopted with flat ends with one-piece windscreens. The units work on branch lines out of Groningen, and carry the logo 'Wadloper'. Literally translated this means 'mud-flat runner' and refers to the terrain of the area.

3100 CLASS   SINGLE UNITS

mBk (DMSO).

Built: 1983.
Builder: Duewag.
Wheel Arrangement: 2 – B.
Engine: Cummins NT855R4 of 210 kW.
Transmission: Hydraulic. Voith T211r.

Accommodation: −/56 1T.
Length over couplings: 22.31 m.
Disc brakes. Magnetic track brakes.

Weight: 36 tonnes.
Max. Speed: 100 km/h.

* Modified for carrying bikes on Harlingenhaven line in summer (−/32 1T).

161	167	173	179	185	3105	3110	3115
162	168	174	180	186	3106	3111	3116
163	169	175	181	3101	3107	3112	3117
164	170	176	182	3102	3108	3113	3118
165	171	177	183	3103	3109	3114	3119
166	172	178	184	3104			

3200 CLASS   2-CAR UNITS

mBk + mBk (DMSO – DMSO).

Built: 1981 − 82.
Builder: Duewag.
Wheel Arrangement: 2 − B + B − 2.
Engine: Cummins NT855R4 of 210 kW (one per car).
Transmission: Hydraulic. Voith T211r.
Accommodation: −/68 1T + −/72.   **Weight:** 35 + 35 tonnes.
Length over couplings: 21.72 + 21.72 m.   **Max. Speed:** 100 km/h.

Disc brakes. Magnetic track brakes.

3201	3205	3209	3213	3217	3221	3225	3228
3202	3206	3210	3214	3218	3222	3226	3229
3203	3207	3211	3215	3219	3223	3227	3230
3204	3208	3212	3216	3220	3224		

DE111 No. 125 at Arnhem on 4th November 1991.   *Mervyn Turvey*

ELECTRIC MULTIPLE UNITS

All NS EMUs are gangwayed within the unit only and have tread brakes except where stated otherwise. All have power-operated sliding or folding doors. Most classes have either a nickname e.g. 'Hondekop' (doghead) or an official name e.g. 'Koploper'.
The various builds of NS EMUs can easily be recognised by their front-end design as follows:
1946 stock ('Mat 46') had a round front and a characteristic green livery. All 1946 stock is now withdrawn from capital stock.
1954 stock ('Mat 54') has a large 'dog head' and was designed for Inter-City and stopping services.
1962 stock ('Mat 62') has a short 'dog head' with the outer cab windows pointed. It is used on stopping services.
Sprinters have a slightly sloping front end which curves in at the bottom.
Railhoppers have ends which slope outwards down to a point below the windscreen and then inwards.
Koplopers have gangwayed ends with a roof cab.
IRM Double-deckers (Regio Runners) have a completely distinctive design.

EMUs are often referred to by their formation code as follows:
EL EMU, D includes guard's/luggage area (dienst), P Post area. 2, 3 or 4 No. of cars.
Example: ELD-2 is a two car EMU with guard's/luggage accommodation.

PLAN Q   HONDEKOP   2-CAR UNITS

1954 stock. These 2-car units are the only ones remaining out of a total build of 67 units. The rest have been withdrawn due to asbestos contamination.

mABDk + mBk (DMBCO – DMSso).

Built: 1958.
Builder-Mech. Parts: Werkspoor.
Builder-Elec. Parts: Smit.
Wheel Arrangement: Bo – 2 + 2 – Bo.
Traction Motors: 4 x 170 kW.
Accommodation: 24/24 1T + – /72 1T.
Weight: 54 + 50 tonnes.
Length over couplings: 25.56 + 25.56 m.
Max. Speed: 140 km/h.

371	374	377	381	384	387	389	392
372	375	378	382	385	388	390	393
373	376	379	383	386			

PLAN V1, V2 & V3   2-CAR UNITS

1962 stock. These sets perform similar duties to the 321 series on local stopping trains on routes such as Amsterdam CS – Arnhem, Rotterdam CS – Nijmegen and Utrecht CS – Leiden.

mABDk + mBk (DMBCO – DMSso).

Built: 1966 – 68.
Builder-Mech. Parts: Werkspoor.
Builder-Elec. Parts: Smit.
Wheel Arrangement: 2 – Bo + Bo – 2.
Traction Motors: 4 x Heemaf of 145 kW.
Accommodation: 24/24 2T + – /80 1T.
Weight: 43 + 42 tonnes.
Length over couplings: 26.07 + 26.07 m.
Max. Speed: 140 km/h.

401 – 415 are plan V1, 416 – 430 are plan V2 and 431 – 438 are plan V3.

401	406	411	416	421	426	431	435
402	407	412	417	422	427	432	436
403	408	413	418	423	428	433	437
404	409	414	419	424	429	434	438
405	410	415	420	425	430		

▲ Class 200 shunter No. 210 at Hoek van Holland on 6th July 1989.   *Eric Sawford*

▼ Class 600 English Electric-built shunter No. 631 seen stabled at Nijmegen on 28th April 1992.
C.L. Booth

▲ The Baldwin-designed Class 1200's main passenger work is on the Zaandvoort-aan-Zee – Maastricht/Heerlen service. 1202 is seen at Utrecht Lunetten with the 17.31 Maastricht – Zandvoort on 19th July 1989. *Peter Fox*

▼ Class 1300 No. 1313, since named 'UITGEEST' at Houten with the 08.54 Zandvoort – Maastricht on 19th July 1989. *Peter Fox*

▲ Class 1600 No. 1623 'HILVERSUM' at Utrecht Lunetten with a cement train on 19th July 1989.
Peter Fox

▼ With the setting up of a separate company for freight work known as NS Cargo comes a new red livery and Class 6400 locos from No. 6511 onwards will carry this livery. No. 6512 is seen at Roosendaal being shunted in a freight train on 5th August 1994. *Peter Fox*

▲ DEII No. 180 at Apeldoorn on 19th July 1989. *Peter Fox*

▼ A four-car rake consisting of two Class 3100s (3101 + 3115) and one Class 3200 (3227) diesel
'Wadloper' diesel-hydraulic units forming the 12.50 Harlingen – Harlingenhaven on 4th August 1994.
No. 3115 has had the seats removed from one end to carry bikes and carries the legend 'Wad-
fietser' on the side, with drawings of bikes. *Peter Fox*

▲ A pair of 3-car sprinters Nos. 2865 + 2859 at Breukelen on 4th August 1994.   *Peter Fox*

▼ Most 1954 stock 'Hondekop' units have now been withdrawn but asbestos-free refurbished sets remain. Unit 757 (then numbered 1757) was seen at Delft Zuid on 29th May 1989 with an Amsterdam – Vlissingen service. this unit is now withdrawn and the Vlissingen service is operated by 'Koplopers'.   *Peter Fox*

▲ ICM 'Koploper' unit 4012 is one of three in 'Aegon' advertising livery and is seen at Utrecht on 18th April 1991. These units will shortly be repainted in standard livery when the advertising contract runs out. *T.N. Hall*

▼ The new SM90 'Railhopper' units have had teething troubles and were undergoing an extensive period of testing when this photo of units 2102 + 2107 was taken at Heerenveen on 4th August 1994, the train being the 10.50 test from Leeuwarden to Steenwijk. *Peter Fox*

▲ One of the new double-deck IRM 'Regio Runner' EMUs at Vlissingen on 5th August 1994. The set is 8204 and the vehicles are 290 8508, 390 8004 and 290 8507. *Peter Fox*

▼ The recently-introduced DD-AR double-deck suburban stock runs in 3 or 4-car formations. Set 7406 is seen at Maarsen on 3rd August 1994 being pushed by Class 1700 No. 1721.*Peter Fox*

Peter Fox

Postal unit 3024 with four of the trailer vans at Maarsen on 3rd August 1994.

▲ An unidentified Benelux push-pull driving trailer at Delft Zuid on the 10.26 Amsterdam – Brussels on 28th May 1989. *Peter Fox*

▼ One of the NS's new buffet cars converted from SNCF Gril-Express coaches at Amsterdam CS forming part of the 14.52 to Port Bon on 3rd August 1994. *Peter Fox*

▲ The new Royal Coach No. 61 84 89-70 003-8 at Den Haag. *Harrie Peters*

▼ Preserved NS No. 1501 (ex BR EM2 No. 27003 DIANA) on show at Rotterdam CS.
David Haydock

▲ The remaining CFL DMUs 201 + 211 and 204 + 206 at Luxembourg depot in February 1994.
David Haydock

▼ EMUs 262 and 254 also at Luxembourg depot on the same occasion.   *David Haydock*

▲ New CFL Z2-type EMU No. 2002 at Noertzange during August 1993. *David C. Rodgers*

▼ Diesel loco 804 shunting at Bettembourg on 10th August 1990. *Andrew Dyson*

▲ 854 acts as Luxembourg works pilot on 12th September 1990.   *C.L. Booth*
▼ 904 at Ettelbruck on 31st May 1989.   *Peter Fox*

▲ 1011 on Luxembourg depot   *David Haydock*

▼ 1032 at Luxembourg station on 25th March 1993.   *T.N. Hall*

▲ OHL trolley 1062 at Noertzange during August 1993. *David C. Rodgers*

▼ Class 1600 No. 1604 'Fond de Gras' stands at Luxembourg with a train for Ettelbruck on 12th September 1990. *C.L. Booth*

CFL

Peter Fox

Class 1800 No. 1803 with Belgian M2 stock at Troisvierges with the 17.50 Luxembourg – Liège on 31st May 1989.

PLAN V4, V5 & V6 2-CAR UNITS

1962 stock. These sets are similar to 401 – 438 but have no luggage compartment. They work very short-distance traffic such as Amsterdam CS – Hoorn/Amersfoort and Utrecht CS – Leiden/Baarn. Amsterdam CS.

mABk + mBk (DMCso – DMSso).

Built: 1969 – 70.
Builder-Mech. Parts: Werkspoor (Talbot*).
Builder-Elec. Parts: Smit.
Wheel Arrangement: 2 – Bo + Bo – 2.
Traction Motors: 4 x Heemaf 145 kW.
Accommodation: 24/40 1T + – /78 1T.
Weight: 43 + 42 tonnes.
Length over couplings: 26.07 + 26.07 m.
Max. Speed: 140 km/h.

441 – 461 are V4, 462 – 471 are V5 and 472 – 483 are V6.

441	447	453	459		464	*	469	*	474	*	479	*
442	448	454	460		465	*	470	*	475	*	480	*
443	449	455	461		466	*	471	*	476	*	481	*
444	450	456	462	*	467	*	472	*	477	*	482	*
445	451	457	463	*	468	*	473	*	478	*	483	*
446	452	458										

PLAN TT 4-CAR UNIT

Prototype unit for 1962 stock. Automatic doors.

Bk + mAD + mB + Bk (DTSso – MBFso – MSO – DTSso).

Built: 1961.
Builder-Mech. Parts: Werkspoor.
Builder-Elec. Parts: Smit.
Wheel Arrangement: 2 – 2 + Bo – Bo + Bo – Bo + 2 – 2.
Traction Motors: 8 x Heemaf 150 kW.
Accommodation: – /80 1T + 41/ – 1T + – /80 1T + – /80 1T.
Weight: 38 + 46 + 44 + 35 tonnes.
Length over couplings: 25.70 + 24.27 + 24.27 + 25.70 m.
Max. Speed: 140 km/h.

501

PLAN T 4-CAR UNITS

These sets operate over a more limited area being normally confined to the Dordrecht – Den Haag – Amsterdam CS line and also the Den Haag – Venlo services which are not loco-hauled.

Bk + mBD + mAB + Bk (DTSso – MBSO(K) – MCso – DTSo).

Built: 1964 – 65.
Builder-Mech. Parts: Werkspoor.
Builder-Elec. Parts: Smit.
Wheel Arrangement: 2 – 2 + Bo – Bo + Bo – Bo + 2 – 2.
Traction Motors: 8 x Heemaf 150 kW.
Accommodation: – /80 1T + 24S 22 buffet 1T + 42/24S 1T + – /80 1T.
Weight: 39 + 47 + 46 + 36 tonnes.
Length over couplings: 26.07 + 24.93 + 24.93 + 26.07 m.
Max. Speed: 140 km/h.

502	506	510	514	518	522	526	529
503	507	511	515	519	523	527	530
504	508	512	516	520	524	528	531
505	509	513	517	521	525		

PLAN P HONDEKOP 4-CAR UNITS

1954 stock. The last remaining units kept because they are asbestos-free. They are used on various secondary services around Den Haag, Rotterdam and Zwolle.

mBk + A + B + mBDk (DMSso – TFso – TSOL(K) – DMBSO).

Built: 1956 – 62.
Builder-Mech. Parts: Werkspoor, Allan & Beijnes.
Builder-Elec. Parts: Smit.
Wheel Arrangement: Bo – Bo + 2 – 2 + 2 – 2 + Bo – Bo.
Traction Motors: 8 x Heemaf 170 kW.
Weight: 57 + 46 + 48 + 55 tonnes.
Length over couplings: 25.56 + 24.07 + 24.07 + 25.56 m.
Max. Speed: 140 km/h.

Refurbished units. Accommodation: – /62 + 48/ – 1T + – /48 22 buffet 2T + – /48 2T. These units have unidirectional 2nd class seating and facing first class seating. They were renumbered 1761 – 1768, but have now reverted to their original numbers to avoid confliction with the new 1700 class locomotives.

| 761 I | 762 I | 763 I | 764 I | 765 I | 766 I | 767 I | 768 I |

Unrefurbished units. Accommodation: – /70 2T + 48/ – 1T + – /56 22 buffet 2T + – /40. These units have facing seats.

| 769 | 770 | 771 | 772 | 774 | |

Refurbished units. Accommodation: – /58 2T + 45/ – 1T + – /48 22 buffet 2T + – /32 2T. These units have unidirectional seating and all-over blue doors. They were also renumbered in the 17xx series. Note: 775/7/8/9 were 1780 – 91 respectively).

| 773 I | 777 I | 779 I | 781 I | 783 I | 784 I | 785 I | 786 I |
| 775 I | 778 I | 780 I | 782 I | | | | |

PLAN V7 2-CAR UNITS

1962 stock. Similar to other plan V units, but with post compartment.

mABk + mBPk (DMCso – DMPSO).

Built: 1970 – 72.
Builder-Mech. Parts: Werkspoor.
Builder-Elec. Parts: Smit.
Wheel Arrangement: 2 – Bo + Bo – 2.
Traction Motors: 4 x Heemaf 145 kW.
Accommodation: 24/40 1T + – /56.
Weight: 43 + 42 tonnes.
Length over couplings: 26.07 + 26.07 m.
Max. Speed: 140 km/h.

801	806	811	816	821	826	831	836
802	807	812	817	822	827	832	837
803	808	813	818	823	828	833	838
804	809	814	819	824	829	834	839
805	810	815	820	825	830	835	840

PLAN V8 – V13 2-CAR UNITS

1962 stock. Talbot version of plan V7.

mABk + mBPk (DMCso – DMPSO).

Built: 1972 – 76.
Builder-Mech. Parts: Talbot.
Builder-Elec. Parts: Smit.
Wheel Arrangement: 2 – Bo + Bo – 2.
Traction Motors: 4 x Heemaf 145 kW.
Accommodation: 24/40 1T + – /56.
Weight: 45 + 43 tonnes.
Length over couplings: 26.07 + 26.07 m.

Max. Speed: 140 km/h.

841	857	873	889	904	919	934	950
842	858	874	890	905	920	935	951
843	859	875	891	906	921	936	952
844	860	876	892	907	922	937	953
845	861	877	893	908	923	939	954
846	862	879	894	909	924	940	955
847	863	880	895	910	925	941	956
848	864	881	896	911	926	942	957
849	865	882	897	912	927	943	958
850	866	883	898	913	928	944	960
851	867	884	899	914	929	945	961
852	868	885	900	915	930	946	962
853	869	886	901	916	931	947	963
854	870	887	902	917	932	948	964
855	871	888	903	918	933	949	965
856	872						

PLAN Y0 (SPRINTER SGM0)   2-CAR UNITS

The earliest batch of 'Sprinter' units from which BR's new DMUs take their name, these sets work on the Zoetermeer Stadslijn which is a circular route through the eastern suburbs of Den Haag. The rapid acceleration from a standing start is especially useful on this line which has stations at very close intervals.

mABk + mBk (DMCO – DMSO).

Built: 1975 – 76.
Builder-Mech. Parts: Talbot.
Builder-Elec. Parts: Oerlikon.
Wheel Arrangement: Bo – Bo + Bo – Bo.
Traction Motors: 8 x Oerlikon 160 kW.
Accommodation: 32/40 + –/72.
Weight: 52.5 + 52.5 tonnes.
Length over couplings: 26.10 + 26.10 m.
Max. Speed: 125 km/h.

Disc brakes.

2001	2003	2005	2007	2009	2011	2013	2015
2002	2004	2006	2008	2010	2012	2014	

PLAN Y1   SPRINTER SGM1   2-CAR UNITS

Similar to plan Y0, but with a toilet and gangways. Similar workings.

mABk + mBk (DMCO – DMSOL).

Built: 1975 – 76.
Builder-Mech. Parts: Talbot.
Builder-Elec. Parts: Oerlikon.
Wheel Arrangement: Bo – Bo + Bo – Bo.
Traction Motors: 8 x Oerlikon 160 kW.
Accommodation: 32/40 + –/72 1T.
Weight: 54 + 53 tonnes.
Length over couplings: 26.10 + 26.10 m.
Max. Speed: 125 km/h.

Disc brakes.

2021	2023	2025	2027	2029	2031	2033	2035
2022	2024	2026	2028	2030	2032	2034	

SM90 RAILHOPPER 2-CAR UNITS

These new EMUs for stopping services went into service early in 1994, but were taken out of service again because of various teething troubles. They feature pressure ventilation and some of them have 2 + 3 second class seating. This has not proved popular with the passengers. At the time of writing they were running tests between Zwolle and Leeuwarden. The composite vehicle has a wheelchair lift.

mABk + mBk (DMCO – DMSO).

Built: 1994.
Builder-Mech. Parts: Talbot.
Builder-Elec. Parts: Holec-Riddekerk.
Wheel Arrangement: Bo – Bo + Bo – Bo.
Traction Motors: 4 Holec 3 phase per car.
Accommodation: 24/41 1T + – /72 (24/47 1T + – /86*).
Weight: 49 + 48 tonnes.
Length over couplings: 26.17 + 26.17 m.
Max. Speed: 160 km/h.

Disc brakes.

2101	2103	2104	2105	2106	2107	2108	2109
2102							

PLAN Y2/Y3(SPRINTER SGM 1/2)3-CAR UNITS

These units are generally confined to workings in the west of the country around Rotterdam and Den Haag and work such turns as Den Haag CS – Leiden – Amsterdam CS, Den Haag CS – Rotterdam CS – Dordrecht – Roosendaal, Den Haag – Rotterdam Hofplein and Rotterdam CS – Hoek van Holland.

mBk + AB + mBk (DMSO – TCO – DMSO).

Built: 1978 – 80/83 – 84*.
Builder-Mech. Parts: Talbot.
Builder-Elec. Parts: Oerlikon.
Wheel Arrangement: Bo – Bo + 2 – 2 + Bo – Bo.
Traction Motors: 8 x Oerlikon 160 kW.
Accommodation: – /72 + 40/40 + – /72 1T.
Weight: 54 + 36 + 53 tonnes.
Length over couplings: 26.15 + 26.40 + 26.15 m.
Max. Speed: 125 km/h.

Disc brakes. 2881 – 2880 were converted from plan Y1 to plan Y2 by the addition of the trailer car and the declassification of the AB (The "first class" seats were similar to the second class ones in any case). 2881 – 2895 are plan Y3.

2836 (2036)	2851 (2051)	2866 (2066)	2881
2837 (2037)	2852 (2052)	2867 (2067)	2882
2838 (2038)	2853 (2053)	2868 (2068)	2883
2839 (2039)	2854 (2054)	2869 (2069)	2884
2840 (2040)	2855 (2055)	2870 (2070)	2885
2841 (2041)	2856 (2056)	2871 (2071)	2886
2842 (2042)	2857 (2057)	2872 (2072)	2887
2843 (2043)	2858 (2058)	2873 (2073)	2888
2844 (2044)	2859 (2059)	2874 (2074)	2889
2845 (2045)	2860 (2060)	2875 (2075)	2890
2846 (2046)	2861 (2061)	2876 (2076)	2891
2847 (2047)	2862 (2062)	2877 (2077)	2892
2848 (2048)	2863 (2063)	2878 (2078)	2893
2849 (2049)	2864 (2064)	2879 (2079)	2894
2850 (2050)	2865 (2065)	2880 (2080)	2895

PLAN mP SINGLE UNIT POSTAL VANS

The crimson and yellow postal units, formerly painted dark red are unique amongst NS units in having conventional drawgear and buffers to facilitate the taking of a trailing load of up to five special four-wheeled postal vans. They can be seen stabled at most of the principal centres during daylight hours as most of their workings occur at night time. There are some daytime workings, however. Their future is in doubt as the NS has lost the postal contract from the now-privatised Dutch post office to road transport from 1996. This may not take place,however.

mP (DMPMV).

Built: 1965 – 66.
Builder-Mech. Parts: Werkspoor.
Builder-Elec. Parts: Smit.
Wheel Arrangement: Bo – Bo.
Traction Motors: 4 x Heemaf 145 kW.
Weight: 54 tonnes.
Length over couplings: 26.40 m.
Max. Speed: 140 km/h.

3001	P	3005	P	3009	P	3014	P	3018	P	3023	P	3027	P	3031	P
3002	P	3006	P	3011	P	3015	P	3019	P	3024	P	3028	P	3033	P
3003	P	3007	P	3012	P	3016	P	3020	P	3025	P	3029	P	3034	P
3004	P	3008	P	3013	P	3017	P	3022	P	3026	P	3030	P	3035	P

PLAN Z0/Z1 (ICM1/2) KOPLOPER 3-CAR UNITS

These striking modern Intercity units, also known as IC3 units, have raised cabs and through gangways. The coaches in these sets formed the basis for the new loco-hauled ICR stock now familiar over many NS routes. The prototype units (4001 – 7) have been modified to standard as far as the basic layout is concerned, but they still retain different interior decor. The units can be found on the Amsterdam CS – Groningen/Leeuwarden and Den Haag/Rotterdam CS – Groningen/Leeuwarden services.

mBDk + AB + sBfk (DMSO (kitchenette/pantry) – TCsoL – DTSOL).

Built: 1977*/83 – 89.
Builder-Mech. Parts: Talbot.
Builder-Elec. Parts: Oerlikon.
Wheel Arrangement: Bo – Bo + 2 – 2 + 2 – 2.
Gangways: Large gangways at both ends with cabs on top.
Traction Motors: 4 x Oerlikon 312 kW.
Accommodation: – /54 + 35/31 2T + – /63 1T + bicycle space.
Weight: 59 + 42 + 42 tonnes.
Length over couplings: 27.05 + 26.50 + 27.05 m.
Max. Speed: 160 km/h.

Disc brakes.
Special Livery: S Aegon advertising livery (white/grey/blue).

4001	I	4016	I	4028	I	4040	I	4052	I	4064	I	4076	I	4087	I
4002	I	4017	I	4029	I	4041	I	4053	I	4065	I	4077	I	4088	I
4003	I	4018	I	4030	I	4042	I	4054	I	4066	I	4078	I	4089	I
4004	I	4019	I	4031	I	4043	I	4055	I	4067	I	4079	I	4090	I
4005	I	4020	I	4032	I	4044	I	4056	I	4068	I	4080	I	4091	I
4006	I	4021	I	4033	I	4045	I	4057	I	4069	I	4081	I	4092	I
4007	I	4022	I	4034	I	4046	I	4058	I	4070	I	4082	I	4093	I
4011	A	4023	I	4035	I	4047	I	4059	I	4071	I	4083	I	4094	I
4012	A	4024	A	4036	I	4048	I	4060	I	4072	I	4084	I	4095	I
4013	I	4025	I	4037	I	4049	I	4061	I	4073	I	4085	I	4096	I
4014	I	4026	I	4038	I	4050	I	4062	I	4074	I	4086	I	4097	I
4015	I	4027	I	4039	I	4051	I	4063	I	4075	I				

PLAN Z2 (ICM3)   KOPLOPER   4-CAR UNITS

These units are a four-car version of the IC3s. Their main uses are Hoofddorp – Enschede, Amsterdam CS – Vlissingen and Rotterdam/Den Haag – Enschede.

mBDk + B + A + sBfk (DMSO (kitchenette/pantry) – MSOL – TFsoL – DTSOL).

Built: 1990 onwards.
Builder-Mech. Parts: Talbot.
Builder-Elec. Parts: Oerlikon.

Wheel Arrangement: Bo − Bo + Bo − 2 + 2 − 2 + 2 − 2.
Gangways: Large gangways at both ends with cabs on top.
Traction Motors: 6 x Oerlikon 312 kW.
Accommodation: −/55 + −/80 1T + 59/− 2T + −/63 1T.
Weight: 59 + 50 + 42 + 42 tonnes.
Length over couplings: 27.05 + 26.50 + 26.50 + 27.05 m.
Max. Speed: 160 km/h.

Disc brakes.

4201 I	4208 I	4215 I	4221 I	4227 I	4233 I	4239 I	4245 I
4202 I	4209 I	4216 I	4222 I	4228 I	4234 I	4240 I	4246 I
4203 I	4210 I	4217 I	4223 I	4229 I	4235 I	4241 I	4247 I
4204 I	4211 I	4218 I	4224 I	4230 I	4236 I	4242 I	4248 I
4205 I	4212 I	4219 I	4225 I	4231 I	4237 I	4243 I	4249 I
4206 I	4213 I	4220 I	4226 I	4232 I	4238 I	4244 I	4250 I
4207 I	4214 I						

PLAN IRM   REGIO RUNNER   3/4-CAR UNITS

These new three and four car double-decker units have just commenced delivery. Each car is numbered separately and a set number is allocated in the 82xx series for three-car units and in the 84xx series for four-car units. Vehicles are listed as though they were 'loose' The set number appears to be determined by the ABv3/4. Thus 8203 contains 390 8003.

mBvk + ABv3/4 (+ ABv5*) + mBvk (DMSO − TCO(− TCO*) − DMSO).

Built: 1994 − 96.
Builder-Mech. Parts: Talbot (De Dietrich*).
Builder-Elec. Parts: Holec-Riddekerk.
Wheel Arrangement: Bo − 2 + 2 − 2 (+ 2 − 2) + Bo − 2.
Traction Motors: 2 x Holec-Riddekerk DMKT 60/45 of 302 kW continuous rating per motor car.
Accommodation: −/93 + 47/42 2T (+ 23/80 2T) + −/93.
Weight: 62.2 + 52.4 (+ 50.4) + 62.2 tonnes.
Length over couplings: 27.05 m.
Max. Speed: 160 km/h.

Disc brakes.

mBvk (DMSO).

290 8501 I	290 8528 I	290 8555 I	290 8582 I	290 8609 I	290 8636 I
290 8502 I	290 8529 I	290 8556 I	290 8583 I	290 8610 I	290 8637 I
290 8503 I	290 8530 I	290 8557 I	290 8584 I	290 8611 I	290 8638 I
290 8504 I	290 8531 I	290 8558 I	290 8585 I	290 8612 I	290 8639 I
290 8505 I	290 8532 I	290 8559 I	290 8586 I	290 8613 I	290 8640 I
290 8506 I	290 8533 I	290 8560 I	290 8587 I	290 8614 I	290 8641 I
290 8507 I	290 8534 I	290 8561 I	290 8588 I	290 8615 I	290 8642 I
290 8508 I	290 8535 I	290 8562 I	290 8589 I	290 8616 I	290 8643 I
290 8509 I	290 8536 I	290 8563 I	290 8590 I	290 8617 I	290 8644 I
290 8510 I	290 8537 I	290 8564 I	290 8591 I	290 8618 I	290 8645 I
290 8511 I	290 8538 I	290 8565 I	290 8592 I	290 8619 I	290 8646 I
290 8512 I	290 8539 I	290 8566 I	290 8593 i	290 8620 I	290 8647 I
290 8513 I	290 8540 I	290 8567 I	290 8594 I	290 8621 I	290 8648 I
290 8514 I	290 8541 I	290 8568 I	290 8595 I	290 8622 I	290 8649 I
290 8515 I	290 8542 I	290 8569 I	290 8596 I	290 8623 I	290 8650 I
290 8516 I	290 8543 I	290 8570 I	290 8597 I	290 8624 I	290 8651 I
290 8517 I	290 8544 I	290 8571 I	290 8598 I	290 8625 I	290 8652 I
290 8518 I	290 8545 I	290 8572 I	290 8599 I	290 8626 I	290 8653 I
290 8519 I	290 8546 I	290 8573 I	290 8600 I	290 8627 I	290 8654 I
290 8520 I	290 8547 I	290 8574 I	290 8601 I	290 8628 I	290 8655 I
290 8521 I	290 8548 I	290 8575 I	290 8602 I	290 8629 I	290 8656 I
290 8522 I	290 8549 I	290 8576 I	290 8603 I	290 8630 I	290 8657 I
290 8523 I	290 8550 I	290 8577 I	290 8604 I	290 8631 I	290 8658 I
290 8524 I	290 8551 I	290 8578 I	290 8605 I	290 8632 I	290 8659 I
290 8525 I	290 8552 I	290 8579 I	290 8606 I	290 8633 I	290 8660 I
290 8526 I	290 8553 I	290 8580 I	290 8607 I	290 8634 I	290 8661 I
290 8527 I	290 8554 I	290 8581 I	290 8608 I	290 8635 I	290 8662 I

ABv3 or Abv4 (TCO).

390 8001 I	390 8015 I	390 8029 I	390 8043 I	390 8056 I	390 8069 I
390 8002 I	390 8016 I	390 8030 I	390 8044 I	390 8057 I	390 8070 I
390 8003 I	390 8017 I	390 8031 I	390 8045 I	390 8058 I	390 8071 I
390 8004 I	390 8018 I	390 8032 I	390 8046 I	390 8059 I	390 8072 I
390 8005 I	390 8019 I	390 8033 I	390 8047 I	390 8060 I	390 8073 I
390 8006 I	390 8020 I	390 8034 I	390 8048 I	390 8061 I	390 8074 I
390 8007 I	390 8021 I	390 8035 I	390 8049 I	390 8062 I	390 8075 I
390 8008 I	390 8022 I	390 8036 I	390 8050 I	390 8063 I	390 8076 I
390 8009 I	390 8023 I	390 8037 I	390 8051 I	390 8064 I	390 8077 I
390 8010 I	390 8024 I	390 8038 I	390 8052 I	390 8065 I	390 8078 I
390 8011 I	390 8025 I	390 8039 I	390 8053 I	390 8066 I	390 8079 I
390 8012 I	390 8026 I	390 8040 I	390 8054 I	390 8067 I	390 8080 I
390 8013 I	390 8027 I	390 8041 I	390 8055 I	390 8068 I	390 8081 I
390 8014 I	390 8028 I	390 8042 I			

ABv5 (TCO)

390 8401 I	390 8409 I	390 8417 I	390 8425 I	390 8433 I	390 8441 I
390 8402 I	390 8410 I	390 8418 I	390 8426 I	390 8434 I	390 8442 I
390 8403 I	390 8411 I	390 8419 I	390 8427 I	390 8435 I	390 8443 I
390 8404 I	390 8412 I	390 8420 I	390 8428 I	390 8436 I	390 8444 I
390 8405 I	390 8413 I	390 8421 I	390 8429 I	390 8437 I	390 8445 I
390 8406 I	390 8414 I	390 8422 I	390 8430 I	390 8438 I	390 8446 I
390 8407 I	390 8415 I	390 8423 I	390 8431 I	390 8439 I	390 8447 I
390 8408 I	390 8416 I	390 8424 I	390 8432 I	390 8440 I	

A rake of six double-decker coaches with a Class 1600 at the end. The first coach is 50 84 26-37 106-0 'Arend'.
Peter Harris

LOCO-HAULED COACHING STOCK
GENERAL

Locomotive hauled coaching stock on the NS is generally referred to by its "plan", which combines the information which in Britain would be provided by the mark and the lot number. The NS type code consists of the "Plan" plus the type code as described in the introductory section of this book.

After A or B comes the number of compartments (or windows in open stock) for each class type, e.g. A4B6 – four first class and six second class compartments.

Four categories of stock are in service:

(a) **Internal stock.** As its title suggests, this stock may only work on NS lines. Train heating is 1000 V 50 Hz and 1500 V d.c. only.
(b) **Buurland stock.** This stock may work into neighbouring countries, i.e. West Germany, Belgium and Luxembourg. Train heating – all voltages.
(c) **Benelux Stock.** This is similar to Buurland stock, but is fitted with jumper cables for push-pull working.
(d) **International stock.** May work anywhere. Train heating – all voltages.

NUMBERING SYSTEM

Loco-hauled coaches are not listed in strict numerical order. It will be seen that the serial numbers of ICR and plan W stock have been chosen so that they do not duplicate one another, although they do duplicate the original double-deckers. The new double deckers have a completely new numbering system which is similar to that used on the IRM 'Regio Runner' EMUs. Coaches are therefore listed in three series, Plan ICR and W, Original double-deckers, New double-deckers and Miscellaneous.

ICR & PLAN W STOCK

ICR is the name given to the new NS Inter-City stock. It comes in three varieties: Internal, Buurland and Benelux. The internal stock has fixed steps, wheras the Buurland and Benelux stock have folding steps. The Benelux stock has jumper cables for push-pull working. All ICR stock has power-operated doors, pressure ventilation, disc brakes and PA. Plan W coaches have been refurbished for use with ICR stock. Plan W1 were used in the original Benelux push-pull sets, whereas plan W2 were for internal use only. All plan W vehicles are now classified as internal .

ICR and W coaches are listed in order of serial number as these do not duplicate.

1 – 500. BENELUX STOCK
PLAN ICR3-A4B6   OPEN COMPOSITE

Built: 1986. Benelux push-pull stock.
Builder: Talbot.   **Accommodation:** 23/48 2T.
Length over Buffers: 26.40 m.   **Weight:** 40 tonnes.
UIC Prefix: 50 84 30-70

061-9 **B**	063-5 **B**	065-0 **B**	066-8 **B**	067-6 **B**	068-4 **B**	071-8 **B**	072-6 **B**
062-7 **B**	064-3 **B**						

PLAN ICR3-Bvk   DRIVING OPEN SECOND

Built: 1986. Benelux push-pull stock.
Builder: Talbot.   **Accommodation:** –/64 1T.
Length over Buffers: 26.40 m.   **Weight:** 41 tonnes.
UIC Prefix: 50 84 28-70

101-7 **B**	103-3 **B**	105-8 **B**	107-4 **B**	108-2 **B**	111-6 **B**	112-4 **B**	113-2 **B**
102-5 **B**	104-1 **B**	106-6 **B**					

PLAN ICR3-B10   OPEN SECOND

Built: 1986 – 87. Benelux push-pull stock.
Builder: Talbot.   **Accommodation:** –/80 1T.
Length over Buffers: 26.40 m.   **Weight:** 40 tonnes.
UIC Prefix: 50 84 20-70

401-9 **B**	404-3 **B**	407-6 **B**	411-8 **B**	413-4 **B**	415-9 **B**	417-5 **B**	421-7 **B**
402-7 **B**	405-0 **B**	408-4 **B**	412-6 **B**	414-2 **B**	416-7 **B**	418-3 **B**	422-5 **B**
403-5 **B**	406-8 **B**						

PLAN ICR4-B10   OPEN SECOND

Built: 1988. Benelux push-pull stock. Formerly Buurland stock.
Builder: Talbot.   **Accommodation:** –/80 1T.
Length over Buffers: 26.40 m.   **Weight:** 40 tonnes.
UIC Prefix: 50 84 20-70

423-3 I	424-1 I	425-8 I	426-6 I	427-4 I

PLAN ICR4-B10   SEMI-OPEN SECOND

Built: 1988. Benelux push-pull stock. Formerly Buurland semi-open firsts.
Builder: Talbot.   **Accommodation:** –/70 1T (24/– in compts, 46/– open).
Length over Buffers: 26.40 m.   **Weight:** 40 tonnes.
UIC Prefix: 50 84 20-70

431-6 I	432-4 I	433-2 I

PLAN W1-B11   OPEN SECOND

Original Benelux push & pull stock. Swivel doors. PA. Renumbered from 50 84 21-30 series. Now used as internal stock on Zandvoort-aan-Zee – Maastricht/Heerlen service.

Built: 1966 – 67.
Builder: Werkspoor.   **Accommodation:** –/88 1T.
Length over Buffers: 26.40 m.   **Weight:** 35 tonnes.
UIC Prefix: 50 84 21-37

451-2 I	454-6 I	457-9 I	462-9 I	465-2 I	468-6 I	473-6 I	476-9 I
452-0 I	455-3 I	458-7 I	463-7 I	466-0 I	471-0 I	474-4 I	477-7 I
453-8 I	456-1 I	461-1 I	464-5 I	467-8 I	472-8 I	475-1 I	

PLAN ICR3-A10   SEMI-OPEN FIRST

Built: 1986. Benelux push-pull stock.
Builder: Talbot.   **Accommodation:** 59/– 1T (24/– in compts, 35/– open).
Length over Buffers: 26.40 m.   **Weight:** 41 tonnes.
UIC Prefix: 50 84 10-70

481-3 **B**	483-9 **B**	485-4 **B**	486-2 **B**	487-0 **B**	488-8 **B**	491-2 **B**	492-0 **B**
482-1 **B**	484-7 **B**						

501 – 999. INTERNAL & 'BUURLAND' STOCK

PLAN W2-B11   OPEN SECOND

Internal stock. Swivel doors. PA.

Built: 1968.
Builder: Werkspoor.   **Accommodation:** –/88 1T.
Length over Buffers: 26.40 m.   **Weight:** 35 tonnes.
UIC Prefix: 50 84 21-37

501-7 I	505-8 I	511-6 I	514-0 I	517-3 I	522-3 I	525-6 I	528-0 I
502-5 I	506-6 I	512-4 I	515-7 I	518-1 I	523-1 I	526-4 I	531-4 I
503-3 I	507-4 I	513-2 I	516-5 I	521-5 I	524-9 I	527-2 I	532-2 I
504-1 I	508-2 I						

PLAN ICR4-A10   SEMI-OPEN FIRST

Built: 1988. Buurland Stock. Through-wired for Benelux service if required. 565 – 7 renumbered from 641 – 691 series.
Builder: Talbot.   **Accommodation:** 59/ – 1T (24/- in compts, 35/ – open).
Length over Buffers: 26.40 m.   **Weight:** 41 tonnes.
UIC Prefix: 50 84 10-70.

564-6 I |565-3 I |566-1 I |567-9 I |

PLAN ICR4-B10   OPEN SECOND

Built: 1988. Buurland Stock. Through-wired for Benelux service if required.
Builder: Talbot.   **Accommodation:** – /80 1T.
Length over Buffers: 26.40 m.   **Weight:** 40 tonnes.
UIC Prefix: 50 84 20-70

571-9 I |572-7 I |573-5 I |574-3 I |575-0 I |

PLAN ICR4-BKD   KITCHEN BRAKE OPEN 2nd

These vehicles consist of a brake open second plus a kitchenette from which a trolley refreshment service operates.

Built: 1988. Buurland Stock. Through-wired for Benelux service if required.
Builder: Talbot.   **Accommodation:** – /49 1T.
Length over Buffers: 26.40 m.   **Weight:** 41 tonnes.
UIC Prefix: 50 84 82-70

591-2 I |592-0 I |593-8 I |

PLAN ICR2-A10   SEMI-OPEN FIRST

Built: 1982 – 84. Internal Stock.
Builder: Talbot.   **Accommodation:** 59/ – 1T. (24/ – in compts, 35/ – open).
Length over Buffers: 26.40 m.   **Weight:** 41 tonnes.
UIC Prefix: 50 84 10-77

601-9 I	605-0 I	611-8 I	615-9 I	621-7 I	625-8 I	631-6 I	635-7 I
602-7 I	606-8 I	612-6 I	616-7 I	622-5 I	626-6 I	632-4 I	636-5 I
603-5 I	607-6 I	613-4 I	617-5 I	623-3 I	627-4 I	633-2 I	637-3 I
604-3 I	608-4 I	614-2 I	618-3 I	624-1 I	628-2 I	634-0 I	

ICR-A10   SEMI-OPEN FIRST

Built: 1981 – 88. Buurland Stock.
Builder: Talbot.   **Accommodation:** 59/ – 1T. (24/ – in compts, 35/ – open).
Length over Buffers: 26.40 m.   **Weight:** 41 tonnes.
UIC Prefix: 50 84 10-70

641 – 646. Plan ICR4. 1988.
651 – 687. Plan ICR1. 1981 – 83.

* Declassified and in international test use. UIC Prefix: 50 84 20 70.

641-2 I	646-1 I	655-2 I	662-8 I	667-7 I	674-3 I	678-4 I	684-2 I
642-0 I	651-1 I	656-0 I	663-6 I	668-5 I	675-0 I	681-8 I	685-9 I
643-8 I	652-9 I	657-8 I	664-4 I	671-9 I	676-8 I	682-6 I	686-7 I
644-6 I	653-7 I	658-6 I	665-1 I	672-7 I	677-6 I	683-4 I	687-5 I
645-3 I	654-5 I	661-0 I	666-9 I	673-5 I			

PLAN ICR2-B10   OPEN SECOND

Built: 1982 – 84. Internal Stock.
Builder: Talbot.   **Accommodation:** – /80 1T.
Length over Buffers: 26.40 m.   **Weight:** 40 tonnes.
UIC Prefix: 50 84 20-77

688-3 I	707-2 I	717-1 I	727-0 I	737-9 I	747-8 I	757-7 I	766-8 I
691-7 I	708-0 I	718-9 I	728-8 I	738-7 I	748-6 I	758-5 I	767-6 I
701-5 I	711-4 I	721-3 I	731-2 I	741-1 I	751-0 I	761-9 I	768-4 I
702-3 I	712-2 I	722-1 I	732-0 I	742-9 I	752-8 I	762-7 I	771-8 I
703-1 I	713-0 I	723-9 I	733-8 I	743-7 I	753-6 I	763-5 I	772-6 I
704-9 I	714-8 I	724-7 I	734-6 I	744-5 I	754-4 I	764-3 I	773-4 I
705-6 I	715-5 I	725-4 I	735-3 I	745-2 I	755-1 I	765-0 I	774-2 I
706-4 I	716-3 I	726-2 I	736-1 I	746-0 I	756-9 I		

PLAN ICR1-B10   SEMI-OPEN SECOND

Built: 1981 – 84. Internal Stock. Rebuilt from Buurland semi-open first 648.
Builder: Talbot.   **Accommodation:** –/70 1T (24/– in compts, 46/– open).
Length over Buffers: 26.40 m.   **Weight:** 40 tonnes.
UIC Prefix: 50 84 20-77

775-9 I |

PLAN ICR1-B10   OPEN SECOND

Built: 1981 – 82. Buurland Stock.
Builder: Talbot.   **Accommodation:** –/80 1T.
Length over Buffers: 26.40 m.   **Weight:** 40 tonnes.
UIC Prefix: 50 84 20-70

801-0 I	811-9 I	821-8 I	831-7 I	841-6 I	848-1 I	857-2 I	866-3 I
802-8 I	812-7 I	822-6 I	832-5 I	842-4 I	851-5 I	858-0 I	867-1 I
803-6 I	813-5 I	823-4 I	833-3 I	843-2 I	852-3 I	861-4 I	868-9 I
804-4 I	814-3 I	824-2 I	834-1 I	844-0 I	853-1 I	862-2 I	871-3 I
805-1 I	815-0 I	825-9 I	835-8 I	845-7 I	854-9 I	863-0 I	872-1 I
806-9 I	816-8 I	826-7 I	836-6 I	846-5 I	855-6 I	864-8 I	873-9 I
807-7 I	817-6 I	827-5 I	837-4 I	847-3 I	856-4 I	865-5 I	874-7 I
808-5 I	818-4 I	828-3 I	838-2 I				

ICR-BKD   KITCHEN BRAKE OPEN SECOND

Buurland stock. These vehicles consist of a brake open second plus a kitchenette from which a trolley refreshment service operates.

Built: 1981 – 88.
Builder: Talbot.   **Accommodation:** –/53 1T (–/49 1T ICR4).
Length over Buffers: 26.40 m.   **Weight:** 41 tonnes.
UIC Prefix: 50 84 82-70

901 – 953. Plan ICR1. 1981 – 82.
954 – 958. Plan ICR4. 1988.

901-3 I	907-0 I	915-3 I	923-7 I	931-0 I	937-7 I	945-0 I	953-4 I
902-1 I	908-8 I	916-1 I	924-5 I	932-8 I	938-5 I	946-8 I	954-2 I
903-9 I	911-2 I	917-9 I	925-2 I	933-6 I	941-9 I	947-6 I	955-9 I
904-7 I	912-0 I	918-7 I	926-0 I	934-4 I	942-7 I	948-4 I	956-7 I
905-4 I	913-8 I	921-1 I	927-8 I	935-1 I	943-5 I	951-8 I	957-5 I
906-2 I	914-6 I	922-9 I	928-6 I	936-9 I	944-3 I	952-6 I	958-3 I

ICR-BKD   KITCHEN BRAKE OPEN 2nd

These vehicles consist of a brake open second plus a kitchenette from which a trolley refreshment service operates.

Built: 1986/8. Benelux push-pull stock.
Builder: Talbot.   **Accommodation:** –/45 1T.
Length over Buffers: 26.40 m.   **Weight:** 41 tonnes.
UIC Prefix: 50 84 82-70

971 – 981. Plan ICR3. 1986.
982. Plan ICR4. 1988. Renumbered from 594.

971-6 **B**	973-2 **B**	975-7 **B**	976-5 **B**	977-3 **B**	978-1 **B**	981-5 **B**	982-3 **B**
972-4 **B**	974-0 **B**						

PLAN DDM1 ORIGINAL DOUBLE-DECKER STOCK

The double-decker stock operates on outer suburban trains on the Amsterdam CS – Den Helder, Amsterdam – Lelystad, Den Haag – Roosendaal – Tilburg and Rotterdam – Amersfoort routes. The Driving coaches are named after endangered species.

DOUBLE DECKER DRIVING OPEN SECOND (Bvs)

Built: 1985 – 86.
Builder: Talbot.
Length over Buffers: 26.89 m.
Accommodation: –/108 1T. (64 upper deck, 44 lower deck).
Weight: tonnes.
UIC Prefix: 50 84 26-37

101-1 Kondor	106-0 Arend	112-8 Cheeta
102-9 Ooievaar	107-8 Zeehond	113-6 Dolfijn
103-7 Bison	108-6 Olifant	114-4 Otter
104-5 Walvis	111-0 Tijger	115-1 Panda
105-2 Neushoorn		

DOUBLE DECKER SECOND (Bv)

Built: 1985 – 86.
Builder: Talbot.
Length over Buffers: 26.40 m.
Accommodation: –/140 1T. (64 upper deck, 76 lower deck).
Weight: tonnes.
UIC Prefix: 50 84 26-37

101-1	107-8	115-1	406-4	414-8	422-1	428-8	435-3
102-9	108-6	401-5	407-2	415-5	423-9	431-2	436-1
103-7	111-0	402-3	408-0	416-3	424-7	432-0	437-9
104-5	112-8	403-1	411-4	417-1	425-4	433-8	438-7
105-2	113-6	404-9	412-2	418-9	426-2	434-6	441-1
106-0	114-4	405-6	413-0	421-3	427-0		

DOUBLE DECKER COMPOSITE (ABv)

Built: 1985 – 86.
Builder: Talbot.
Length over Buffers: 26.40 m.
Accommodation: 64/60 1T. (32/24 upper deck, 32/36 lower deck).
Weight: tonnes.

UIC Prefix: 50 84 26-37

601-0	605-1	611-9	615-0	621-8	625-9	628-3	633-3
602-8	606-9	612-7	616-8	622-6	626-7	631-7	634-1
603-6	607-7	613-5	617-6	623-4	627-5	632-5	635-8
604-4	608-5	614-3	618-4	624-2			

NEW DOUBLE-DECKER STOCK TYPE DD – AR

This new double-decker stock works in suburban trains all around the Randstad area. (local services). The numbering system strays away from the normally mandatory UIC system. The coaches work in sets of nominal fixed formation consisting of a Class 1700 locomotive, a composite, one or two seconds and a driving second. The set numbers consist of a '7', a digit denoting the number of cars and the last two digits of the driving trailer. Thus 7345 would be a three car set with the driving trailer 7045. Formations are changed from time to time. Fifty power cars are on order and these will convert 50 of the sets to EMUs! The Class 1700s released will then be used to replace Classes 1100 and 1200 and possibly 1300.

DOUBLE DECKER DRIVING OPEN SECOND (Bvs)

Built: 1992 – 94.
Builder: Talbot.

Length over Buffers: 26.89 m.
Accommodation: −/120 1T. (64 upper deck, 52 lower deck and 4 in ends).
Weight: 53 tonnes.

270 7001 − 33 are plan DDM2, and 270 7034 − 79 are plan DDM3.

270 7001	270 7015	270 7028	270 7041	270 7054	270 7067
270 7002	270 7016	270 7029	270 7042	270 7055	270 7068
270 7003	270 7017	270 7030	270 7043	270 7056	270 7069
270 7004	270 7018	270 7031	270 7044	270 7057	270 7070
270 7005	270 7019	270 7032	270 7045	270 7058	270 7071
270 7006	270 7020	270 7033	270 7046	270 7059	270 7072
270 7007	270 7021	270 7034	270 7047	270 7060	270 7073
270 7008	270 7022	270 7035	270 7048	270 7061	270 7074
270 7009	270 7023	270 7036	270 7049	270 7062	270 7075
270 7010	270 7024	270 7037	270 7050	270 7063	270 7076
270 7011	270 7025	270 7038	270 7051	270 7064	270 7077
270 7012	270 7026	270 7039	270 7052	270 7065	270 7078
270 7013	270 7027	270 7040	270 7053	270 7066	270 7079
270 7014					

DOUBLE DECKER SECOND (Bv)

Built: 1992 − 94.
Builder: Talbot.
Length over Buffers: 26.40 m.
Accommodation: −/140 1T. (64 upper deck, 64 lower deck and 12 in ends).
Weight: 46 tonnes.

280 7201 − 50 are plan DDM2, and 280 7251 − 7302 are plan DDM3.

280 7201	280 7218	280 7235	280 7252	280 7269	280 7286
280 7202	280 7219	280 7236	280 7253	280 7270	280 7287
280 7203	280 7220	280 7237	280 7254	280 7271	280 7288
280 7204	280 7221	280 7238	280 7255	280 7272	280 7289
280 7205	280 7222	280 7239	280 7256	280 7273	280 7290
280 7206	280 7223	280 7240	280 7257	280 7274	280 7291
280 7207	280 7224	280 7241	280 7258	280 7275	280 7292
280 7208	280 7225	280 7242	280 7259	280 7276	280 7293
280 7209	280 7226	280 7243	280 7260	280 7277	280 7294
280 7210	280 7227	280 7244	280 7261	280 7278	280 7295
280 7211	280 7228	280 7245	280 7262	280 7279	280 7296
280 7212	280 7229	280 7246	280 7263	280 7280	280 7297
280 7213	280 7230	280 7247	280 7264	280 7281	280 7298
280 7214	280 7231	280 7248	280 7265	280 7282	280 7299
280 7215	280 7232	280 7249	280 7266	280 7283	280 7300
280 7216	280 7233	280 7250	280 7267	280 7284	280 7301
280 7217	280 7234	280 7251	280 7268	280 7285	280 7302

DOUBLE DECKER COMPOSITE (ABv)

Built: 1992 − 94.
Builder: Talbot.
Length over Buffers: 26.40 m.
Accommodation: 64/60 1T. (32/24 upper deck, 32/24 lower deck and 12 in ends).
Weight: 46 tonnes.

380 7501 − 33 are plan DDM2, and 380 7534 − 77 are plan DDM3.

380 7501	380 7510	380 7519	380 7528	380 7537	380 7546
380 7502	380 7511	380 7520	380 7529	380 7538	380 7547
380 7503	380 7512	380 7521	380 7530	380 7539	380 7548
380 7504	380 7513	380 7522	380 7531	380 7540	380 7549
380 7505	380 7514	380 7523	380 7532	380 7541	380 7550
380 7506	380 7515	380 7524	380 7533	380 7542	380 7551
380 7507	380 7516	380 7525	380 7534	380 7543	380 7552
380 7508	380 7517	380 7526	380 7535	380 7544	380 7553
380 7509	380 7518	380 7527	380 7536	380 7545	380 7554

380 7555	380 7559	380 7563	380 7567	380 7571	380 7575
380 7556	380 7560	380 7564	380 7568	380 7572	380 7576
380 7557	380 7561	380 7565	380 7569	380 7573	380 7577
380 7558	380 7562	380 7566	380 7570	380 7574	

MISCELLANEOUS STOCK
PLAN E-Df   BICYCLE BRAKE

Built: 1958 as post office vehicles. Converted 1989–93 to carry cycles. Used in summer on Zandvoort-aan-Zee – Maastricht service.
Builder: Werkspoor.
Length over Buffers: 23.05 m.
Accommodation: – /4.
Weight: 45 tonnes.

50 84 92-37 001-2 (50 84 87-37 202-3)	50 84 92-37 005-9 (50 84 87-37 216-3)
50 84 92-37 002-0 (50 84 87-37 213-0)	50 84 92-37 006-7 (50 84 87-37 222-1)
50 84 92-37 003-8 (50 84 87-37 225-4)	50 84 92-37 007-5 (50 84 87-37 212-2)
50 84 92-37 004-6 (50 84 87-37 226-2)	50 84 92-37 008-3 (50 84 87-37 206-4)

COUCHETTES

Ex DB. Part of NS/DB pool.

Built: 1962 onwards.
Builders: Various.
Length over Buffers: 26.40 m.
Accommodation: – /60 2T 4W.
Weight: 39 tonnes.
Max. Speed: 140 km/h.

51 84 50-30 009-1 (51 80 50-30 036-8)	51 84 50-30 015-8 (51 80 50-30 056-6)
51 84 50-30 010-9 (51 80 50-30 038-4)	51 84 50-30 016-6 (51 80 50-30 065-7)
51 84 50-30 011-7 (51 80 50-30 048-3)	51 84 50-30 017-4 (51 80 50-30 071-5)
51 84 50-30 013-3 (51 80 50-30 049-1)	51 84 50-30 018-2 (51 80 50-30 079-8)
51 84 50-30 012-5 (51 80 50-30 051-7)	51 84 50-30 019-0 (51 80 50-30 084-8)
51 84 50-30 014-1 (51 80 50-30 054-1)	51 84 50-30 020-8 (51 80 50-30 020-2)

UNIVERSAL SLEEPING CAR

Built: .
Builder: .
Length over Buffers: .
Berths: 30.
Weight: tonnes.
Max Speed: 160 km/h.

71 84 70-70 016-9	71 84 70-70 018-5	71 84 70-70 020-1
71 84 70-70 017-7	71 84 70-70 019-3	

TYPE WR   RESTAURANT CAR

International stock. Ex SNCF Gril-Express. Full details not available.

Built:
Builder:
Length over Buffers: 24.5 m.
Accommodation: 22 chairs.
Weight: 54 tonnes.
Max Speed: 160 km/h.

61 84 88-70 015-3	61 84 88-70 021-1 (61 87 88 90 134-5)
61 84 88-70 016-1	61 84 88-70 022-9 (61 87 88 90 114-7)
61 84 88-70 017-9	61 84 88-70 023-7 (61 84 88 70 131-5)
61 84 88-70 018-7	61 84 88-70 024-5 (61 84 88 70 143-0)
61 84 88-70 019-5	61 84 88-70 025-2 (61 84 88 70 148-9)
61 84 88-70 020-3 (61 87 88 90 145-1)	61 84 88-70 026-0 (61 84 88 70 127-3)

COUCHETTES

Ex TUI. Full details not available.
Built:
Builder:
Length over Buffers:
Berths: 55.
Weight: 53 tonnes.
Max Speed: 200 km/h.

61 84 50-90 101-1 (61 80 50-90 101-5)	61 84 50-90 106-0 (61 80 50-90 106-4)
61 84 50-90 102-9 (61 80 50-90 102-3)	61 84 50-90 107-8 (61 80 50-90 107-2)
61 84 50-90 103-7 (61 80 50-90 103-1)	61 84 50-90 108-6 (61 80 50-90 108-0)
61 84 50-90 104-5 (61 80 50-90 104-9)	61 84 50-90 109-4 (61 80 50-90 109-8)
61 84 50-90 105-2 (61 80 50-90 105-6)	

COUCHETTES

Ex TUI. Full details not available.
Built:
Builder:
Length over Buffers:
Berths: 55.
Weight: 51 tonnes.
Max Speed: 160 km/h.

61 84 50-70 110-2 (61 80 50-70 110-0)	61 84 50-70 121-3 (61 80 50-70 121-7)
61 84 50-70 111-4 (61 80 50-70 111-8)	61 84 50-70 122-1 (61 80 50-70 122-5)
61 84 50-70 112-2 (61 80 50-70 112-6)	61 84 50-70 123-9 (61 80 50-70 123-3)
61 84 50-70 113-0 (61 80 50-70 113-4)	61 84 50-70 124-7 (61 80 50-70 124-1)
61 84 50-70 115-5 (61 80 50-70 115-9)	61 84 50-70 125-4 (61 80 50-70 125-8)
61 84 50-70 116-3 (61 80 50-70 116-7)	61 84 50-70 126-2 (61 80 50-70 126-6)
61 84 50-70 117-1 (61 80 50-70 117-5)	61 84 50-70 127-0 (61 80 50-70 127-4)
61 84 50-70 118-9 (61 80 50-70 118-3)	61 84 50-70 128-8 (61 80 50-70 128-2)
61 84 50-70 119-7 (61 80 50-70 119-1)	61 84 50-70 129-6 (61 80 50-70 129-0)
61 84 50-70 120-5 (61 80 50-70 120-9)	61 84 50-70 130-4 (61 80 50-70 130-8)

ROYAL SALOONS

Originally composites. Rebuilt as Royal saloons 1955/53. . . .001 was built for Queen Juliana and consists of a toilet, bathroom, bedroom, full width lounge, coupé, kitchen and attendant's compartment with boiler. . . .002 was built for Prince Bernhard and Princess Beatrix and consists of two bedrooms, two bathrooms, a combined sitting room and bedroom, an attendant's compartment with boiler and a governess' compartment.

Built: 1932.
Builder: Werkspoor.
Length over Buffers: 21.80 m.
Weight: 56 (53*) tonnes.

61 84 89-30 001-1　　　(9)　|61 84 89-30 002-9　　　(8)* |

ROYAL SALOON

Converted: 1994 from plan ICR4-A10 semi-open first 50 84 10-70 647-9 built 1988.
Builder: Talbot.　　　　　　**Length over Buffers:** 26.40 m.
Weight: 41 tonnes.

61 84 89-70 003-8

SLEEPING CAR TYPE Mü

Built: 1973.
Builder: Fiat.
Length over Buffers: 28.40 m.
Berths: 36. Convertible first/second.
Weight: 55 tonnes.

71 84 72-80 622-0 |

SLEEPING CAR TYPE T2S

Built: 1975.
Builder:
Length over Buffers: 26.40 m.
Berths: 34. (17 twin berth compartments).
Weight: 55 tonnes.

71 84 75-70 458-8 |71 84 75-70 459-6 |

DEPARTMENTAL VEHICLES

80 84 978-1 002-4	Ultrasonic test unit (diesel hydraulic)
60 84 978-1 005-1	CTO test vehicle.
80 84 978-1 602-1	mDw ATB test car ('Jules')
80 84 978-1 805-0	

Plan W2 open second 50 84 21-37 523-1 at Maastricht on 6th August 1994.   *Peter Fox*

NS PRESERVED LOCOMOTIVES
& MULTIPLE UNITS

STEAM LOCOMOTIVES:

Number	Wheels	Built	Status	Location
13	2 – 4 – 0	1865	M	Utrecht
89	2 – 4 – 0	1880	M	Utrecht
107	4 – 4 – 0	1889	M	Utrecht
326	2 – 4 – 0	1881	M	Utrecht
2104	4 – 4 – 0	1914	M	Utrecht
3737	4 – 6 – 0	1911	M	Utrecht
5085	2 – 10 – 0	1945	M	Utrecht
6317	4 – 8 – 4T	1931	M	Utrecht
7742	0 – 6 – 0T	1914	MA	SHM
8811	0 – 6 – 0ST	1943	M	SSN
8815	0 – 6 – 0ST	1943	MR	UK
8817	0 – 6 – 0ST	1943	P	Autotron Rosmalen
8826	0 – 6 – 0ST	1943	P	Tilburg
657	0 – 4 – 0T	1901	MA	MBS

DIESEL & ELECTRIC LOCOMOTIVES:

Number	Wheels	Built	Status	Location
103	B pm	1931	M	Utrecht
116	B pm	1931	MR	VSM Beekbergen
137	B pm	1929	M	Utrecht
197	B pm	1932	M	MBS
251	Bo de	1935	MA	SGB. Goes
293	Bo de	1938	MA	MBS Haaksbergen
311	B de	1940	MA	Utrecht
451	C de	1956	MA	MBS
508	C de	1944	MS	Utrecht (stored at Blerick)
512	C de	1944	M	Leuvehaven, Rotterdam
532	C de	1954	MA	VSM
636	C de	1956	MA	VSM Beekbergen
640	C de	1956	MA	ZLSM STIBANS. Utrecht
1010	1A – Bo – A1 e	1949	M	STIBANS. Utrecht
1125	Bo – Bo e	1951	M	Utrecht. Restored as 1122
1501	Co – Co e	1954	MA	Feijenoord
1502	Co – Co e	1954	MA	Midland Railway Trust, Butterley, UK. Now BR 27000
1505	Co – Co e	1954	M	Greater Manchester, UK
2498	Bo – Bo de	1955	M	Utrecht

DIESEL & ELECTRIC RAILCARS:

Number	Wheels	Built	Status	Location
20	Bo – Bo DEMU	1954	M	Utrecht
27	3-car DEMU	1934	M	Utrecht
41	Bo – Bo DMU	1935	M	Utrecht (Stored at Blerick)
252	2-car EMU	1950	MS	STIBANS. Roosendaal
273	4-car EMU	1952	MS	Utrecht
9107	Bo – Bo EMU	1924	MA	Utrecht. ('De Blokkendoos' box of bricks).
8104	EMU dt	1924	MA	Utrecht. (Driving Trailer for above).
9952	EMU		MR	Utrecht. To arrive ex -Germany.

Ex DB/DR LOCOMOTIVES PRESERVED IN THE NETHERLANDS

Number	Wheels	Built	Status	Location
01.1075	4 – 6 – 2	1937	MR	SSN
23.023	2 – 6 – 2	1952	MA	SSN
23.071	2 – 6 – 2	1956	MA	VSM
23.076	2 – 6 – 2	1956	MA	VSM
41.105	2 – 8 – 2	1939	MA	SSN
50.1255	2 – 10 – 0	1941	MR	SSN
50.3564	2 – 10 – 0	1940	MA	VSM
50.3654	2 – 10 – 0	1942	MA	VSM
50.3681	2 – 10 – 0	1940	MS	VSM
52.3879	2 – 10 – 0	1944	MA	SSN
52.8053	2 – 10 – 0	1943	MA	VSM
52.8139	2 – 10 – 0	1944	M	VSM
64.415	2 – 6 – 2T	1936	MA	SSN
65.018	2 – 8 – 4T	1956	MA	SSN
80.036	0 – 6 – 0T	1929	MA	VSM
94.640	0 – 10 – 0T	1923	P	Gennep

For status codes see SNCB section, and for society and railway abbreviations see the "Museums and Museum Lines" section.

Plan E bicycle brake No. 50 84 92-37 008-7 at Maastricht on 6th august 1994.   *Peter Fox*

3. LUXEMBOURG RAILWAYS (CFL)

Luxembourg Railways are known by the abbreviation CFL (Société Nationale des Chemins de Fer Luxembourgeois). The total length of the system is only 270 km, but this does not mean that the network is uninteresting. The CFL operates locomotives and multiple units of types that are also found in neighbouring countries, and the city of Luxembourg also sees through workings of locomotives from the DB, SNCB and SNCF. Electrification is at 25 kV a.c. and all CFL electric locomotives and multiple units operate on this system. SNCB/NMBS 3000 V d.c. electircs can also run into Luxembourg station.

NUMBERING SYSTEM

The CFL loco numbering system is based on the horse power of the locomotives. 1801 is an 1800 hp locomotive, whilst 3620 is one of 3600 hp. However, departmental vehicles are numbered 10XX whilst the new Z2 EMUs are numbered 20XX.

DEPOTS AND WORKSHOPS

With such a compact system there is no need for many depots. All locomotives are allocated to Luxembourg shed. There are stabling points at Ettelbruck, Wasserbillig, Troisvierges, Bettembourg Yard, Pétange and Esch sur Alzette. Locomotives also stable overnight at the various branch termini as required. Because of the small fleet only one workshop is required and this is located opposite the station at Luxembourg.

DEVELOPMENTS

In 1993, CFL completed electirification of its network at 25 kV a.c. 50 Hz, except for the line to Arlon (B), electrified at 3000 V d.c. and short freight branches Kleinbettingen – Steinfort and Schieren – Bissen, which remain diesel worked. As this book went to press, Westwaggon Class 200 railcars and General Motors Class 1600 diesels were due to be withdrawn, replaced on the Trier line by DB Class 628.4 DMUs. CFL has bought two of these units, but they will be used in a pool and be maintained by DB. They therefore will appear in the Platform 5 German Railways book. In future, the whole loco fleet will be replaced by 30 dual-voltage (3000 V d.c./25 kV a.c.) Bo – Bo electrics to be ordered in 1994 jointly with SNCB. Until these are delivered in 1996 – 7, the fleet is likely to stay stable.

DIESEL MULTIPLE UNITS
CLASS 200   2-CAR UNITS

These vehicles were originally numbered 201A/201B etc. Note that on DMUs the numbers refer to the car, whereas on EMUs the numbers refer to the complete unit. These units should be withdrawn late 1994. CFL will probably keep one as a ''historic unit''.

B + B (DMSO – DMSO).

Built: 1956.
Builder: Westwaggon.
Wheel Arrangement: 1A – 2 + 2 – A1.
Engine: Deutz A12L614 of 149 kW (one per car).
Transmission: Hydraulic. Voith.
Accommodation: – /94 1T + – /94 1T.
Total Weight: 31.5 + 31.5 tonnes.
Length over Couplings: 23.72 + 23.72 m.
Max. Speed: 105 km/h.

201 211 |204 206 |218 (S)

CFL NETWORK MAP

ELECTRIC MULTIPLE UNITS
CLASS 250   2-CAR UNITS

These are based on similar units supplied to the SNCF and feature monomotor bogies and thyristor control. Up to three units may work in multiple within the class and with Class 260.

AB + BD (DMCO – DMBSO).

Built: 1975.
Builder-Mech. Parts: CF.
Builder-Elec. Parts: MTE, CEM.
Wheel Arrangement: 2 – B + 2 – 2.
Traction Motors: 1 x GRLM 792 B of 615 kW.
Accommodation: 14/80 1T + – /74.
Total Weight: 79.5 tonnes.
Length over couplings: 25.325 + 25.325 m.
Max. Speed: 120 km/h.

| 251 | 252 | 253 | 254 | 255 | 256 |

CLASS 260   3-CAR UNITS

These units were acquired second-hand from the SNCF and were previously Z 6168/9 respectively. The centre cars can operate in 250 class. There is only one diagram which works mainly Dudelange and Diekirch branches.

BD + B + AB (DMBSO – TSO – DTCO).

Built: 1970.
Builder-Mech. Parts: CF/Alsthom.
Builder-Elec. Parts: CEM.
Wheel Arrangement: 2 – B + 2 – 2 + 2 – 2.
Traction Motors: 1 x GRLM 792 B of 615 kW.
Accommodation: – /79 + – /107 + 16/71 1T.
Total Weight: 52 + 27 + 29 tonnes.
Length over couplings: 25.325 + 23.8 + 25.325 m.
Max. Speed: 120 km/h.

| 261 | 262 |

CLASS 2000   2-CAR UNITS

These EMUs are similar to SNCF Class Z 11500 and they inter-work with SNCF Z 11500 units based just across the frontier at Thionville reaching Longwy and even Nancy.

ABD + B (DMBCO – DTSO).

Built: 1990 – 92.
Builders: De Dietrich/ANF/Alsthom.
Wheel Arrangement: Bo – Bo + 2 – 2.
Traction Motors: 4 x TAB 676 B1 of 305 kW each.
Accommodation: 24/43 1T + – /84 1T.
Weight: 64 + 40 tonnes.
Length over couplings: 25.10 + 25.10 m.
Max. Speed: 160 km/h.

2001	2004	2007	2010	2013	2016	2019	2021
2002	2005	2008	2011	2014	2017	2020	2022
2003	2006	2009	2012	2015	2018		

2018 is named TROISVIERGES.

DIESEL LOCOMOTIVES

Note: Self-propelled departmental vehicles are also numbered in this series.

CLASS 800   Bo – Bo

These locos are unique to the CFL and are typical American switches of the early 1950s. They are used for shunting and trip working at Bettembourg and Luxembourg Triage.

Built: 1954.
Builder: AFB.
Engine: GM 8-567B of 600 kW at 835 rpm.
Transmission: Electric. Four GM 4-EMD-D27B axle-hung traction motors.
Train Heating: None   **Weight in Full Working Order:** 74 tonnes.
Maximum Tractive Effort: 179 kN.   **Length over Buffers:** 13.795 m.
Driving Wheel Dia.: 1050 mm.   **Max. Speed:** 80 km/h.

801 |802 |803 |804 |805 |806

CLASS 850   Bo – Bo

These are from the same family as SNCF Class BB 63500. Used on station pilot and trip freight duties.

Built: 1956 – 57.
Builder: BL.
Engine: SACM MGO V12SH of 615 kW at 1500 rpm.
Transmission: Electric. Four BL 453-29B axle-hung traction motors.
Train Heating: None.   **Weight in Full Working Order:** 72 tonnes.
Maximum Tractive Effort: 174 kN.   **Length over Buffers:** 14.75 m.
Driving Wheel Dia.: 1100 mm.   **Max. Speed:** 105 km/h.

851 |852 |853 |854 |855 |856 |857 |858

CLASS 900   Bo – Bo

Very similar to Class 850 with same duties.

Built: 1958.
Builder: BL.
Engine: SACM MGO V12SHR of 690 kW at 1500 rpm.
Transmission: Electric. Four BL 453-29D axle-hung traction motors.
Train Heating: None.   **Weight in Full Working Order:** 72 tonnes.
Maximum Tractive Effort: 174 kN.   **Length over Buffers:** 14.75 m.
Driving Wheel Dia.: 1100 mm.   **Max. Speed:** 105 km/h.

901 |903 |905 |907 |909 |911 |912 |913
902 |904 |906 |908 |910

902 is named STEINFORT.

CLASS 1000   B

Used for light shunting duties and usually found at Bettembourg p.w. Depot, Luxembourg and Ettelbruck.

Built: 1972.
Builder: Jung.
Engine: Deutz F12 L413 of 186 kW at 2150 rpm.
Transmission: Hydraulic. Voith L2r4SU2.
Train Heating: None   **Weight in Full Working Order:** 32 tonnes.
Maximum Tractive Effort: 94 kN.   **Length over Buffers:** 7.20 m.
Driving Wheel Dia.: 950 mm.   **Max. Speed:** 60 km/h.

1001 |1002 |1003 |1004 |

CLASS 1010   B

This shunter has an auto-coupler, it is usually found at Luxembourg depot.

Built: 1964.

Builder: Henschel.
Engine: Henschel 6R 1215A of 160 kW at 1800 rpm.
Transmission: Hydraulic. Voith DIWABUS 200S/355.

Train Heating: None	**Weight in Full Working Order:** 22 tonnes.
Maximum Tractive Effort: 64 kN.	**Length over Buffers:** 7.10 m.
Driving Wheel Dia.: 850 mm.	**Max. Speed:** 24 km/h.

1011 (2011)

CLASS 1020   B

Used for light shunting duties, usually 1021 at Luxembourg shed, 1022 at Luxembourg Works. 1023/4 are fitted with auto-couplers and are used at Pétange Wagon Works.

Built: 1952 – 57.
Builder: Deutz.
Engine: Deutz A8 L614 of 100 kW at 1800 rpm.
Transmission: Hydraulic. Voith L33Y.

Train Heating: None	**Weight in Full Working Order:** 22 tonnes.
Maximum Tractive Effort: 64 kN.	**Length over Buffers:** 7.57 m.
Driving Wheel Dia.: 850 mm.	**Max. Speed:** 53 km/h.

1021 |1022 |1023 |1024 |

CLASS 1030   B

1031 is fitted with remote control. It is used by the track department.

Built: 1988.
Builder: Jenbacher Werke, Austria.
Engine: MTU 8V 183 TA12 of 267 kW at 2200 rpm.
Transmission: Hydraulic. Voith L2r4SV2.

Train Heating: None	**Weight in Full Working Order:** 36 tonnes.
Maximum Tractive Effort: 117 kN.	**Length over Buffers:** 8.55 m.
Driving Wheel Dia.: 950 mm.	**Max. Speed:** 60 km/h.

1031 |1032 |1033

CLASS 1050   P.W. TROLLEYS

These permanent way trolleys have a large cabin at one end for the driver and staff and a hydraulic arm at the other. 1051 was formerly numbered departmental 10.

Built: 1980 – 82.
Builder: Donelli/Geismar.
Engine: Deutz F8 L413F of 173.5 kW. at 1500 rpm.
Transmission: Hydraulic. Clark R 28624-9.

Length over Buffers: 9.90 m.	**Weight in Full Working Order:** 36 tonnes.
Driving Wheel Dia.: 850 mm.	**Max. Speed:** 80 km/h.

1051 |1052 |1053 |1054 |

CLASS 1060   O.H.L. TROLLEYS

This is another departmental vehicle numbered in the capital stock series. It features a dummy pantograph and a working area above the crew accommodation. It is used for overhead line maintenance.

Built: 1985.
Builder: Donelli/Geismar.
Transmission: Hydromechanical. MHR 28628-2.

Engine: Deutz F8 L413F of 173.5 kW at 1500 rpm.

Length over Buffers: 12.14 m.	**Weight in Full Working Order:** 24 tonnes.
Driving Wheel Dia.: 850 mm.	**Max. Speed:** 80 km/h.

1061 |1062

CLASS 1070   O.H.L. TROLLEYS

A "motorised wagon". Can operate on its own at 5 km/h but is usually coupled to 1062. 1071

CLASS 1600   Co – Co

Very similar to SNCB Class 52. The Class is scheduled for early withdrawal although 1604 will be retained as a "historic monument". this information is carried on a very verbose nameplate.

Built: 1955.
Builder-Mech. Parts: AFB.
Builder-Elec. Parts: GM.
Engine: GM 16-567C of 1265 kW at 835 rpm.
Transmission: Electric. 6 SMIT D19 axle-hung traction motors.
Train Heating: Steam. Vapor OK4616.   **Weight in Full Working Order:** 108 tonnes.
Maximum Tractive Effort: 245 kN.   **Length over Buffers:** 19.007 m.
Driving Wheel Dia.: 1010 mm.   **Max. Speed:** 120 km/h.

1602	1604 FOND-DE-GRAS
1603	

CLASS 1800   Co – Co

Identical to SNCB Class 55 except for the coupling of traction motors. 12 of the class are diagrammed, mainly on freights between Stockem yard in Belgium and Bettembourg yard or through to Thionville or Metz in France. In 1993, a pair started working freights from Athus to Ronet near Namur. Boilered locos also haul some passenger, mainly to Troisvierges but also to Kleinbettingen.

Built: 1963/4.
Builder-Mech. Parts: BN.
Builder-Elec. Parts: ACEC/SEM.
Engine: GM 16-567C of 1435 kW at 835 rpm.
Transmission: Electric. Six ACEC DS7 axle-hung traction motors.
Train Heating: Steam. Vapor OK 4616.   **Weight in Full Working Order:** 110 (114 s) tonnes.
Maximum Tractive Effort: 272 kN.   **Length over Buffers:** 19.55 m.
Driving Wheel Dia.: 1010 mm.   **Max. Speed:** 120 km/h.

Rheostatic braking.
s – Steam heating fitted.

1801	s		1811		ETTELBRUCK
1802	s	Blankenberge	1812		
1803	s		1813		Schieren
1804	s		1814		
1805	s	MONDORF-LES-BAINS	1815	s	KAUTENBACH 1881 – 1981
1806		COMMUNE DE WALFERDANGE	1816	s	LAROCHETTE
1807		COMMUNE DE PÉTANGE	1817	s	
1808			1818	s	
1809			1819	s	PRINCE HENRI
1810			1820	s	Bettembourg

ELECTRIC LOCOMOTIVES
CLASS 3600   Bo – Bo

These 25 kV a.c. electric locos are similar to SNCF Class BB 12000. 14 locos are diagrammed, mainly on freight over the Bettembourg – Esch – Rodange line, generated by the steelworks at Belval. Peak periods see 5 or 6 locos on passenger trains covering most lines.

Built: 1958 – 59.
Builder-Mech. Parts: MTE.
Builder-Elec. Parts: MTE.
Traction Motors: Four SW 435.
One Hour Rating: 2650 kW.   **Total Weight:** 84 tonnes.
Maximum Tractive Effort: 186 kN.   **Length over Buffers:** 15.20 m.
Driving Wheel Dia.: 1250 mm.   **Max. Speed:** 120 km/h.

3601		3611	
3602		3612	
3603		3613	GUILLAUME LUXEMBOURG
3604		3614	RUMELANGE
3605		3616	DUDELANGE
3606		3617	
3607	ESCH/ALZETTE	3618	WILTZ
3608	LORENTZWEILER	3619	WASSERBILLIG
3609		3620	REISERBANN
3610			

HAULED COACHING STOCK

There were originally four types of coaching stock vehicles in use on the CFL, types B, AB and BD and ABD. The ABD vehicles were identical to the BD vehicles and the AB vehicles were identical to the B vehicles, except for the upholstery on the first class seats.

Since these vehicles were built, many have been renumbered more than once and some have been modified. In particular, there will in future only be two types, B (SO) and ABD (BCO). In order to sort out the renumbering, it helps to use the pre-UIC number as a reference. The build details of these were as follows: 2101 – 36 type B12, 2137 – 38 A3B9, 2161 – 69 A3B9, 2181 – 93 B9D. The serial number of the vehicle is digits 10 – 12 of the UIC number. The first of these digits changes from a '3' to a '4' and vice-versa when the coaches are shopped, depending on whether 120 or 140 km/h bogies are fitted. Thus the list is in the order of the last two digits of the serial number. In the list which follows, three numbers are quoted:

1. The present UIC number.
2. The UIC number shown in 'Benelux Locomotives and Coaching Stock 3rd edition'.
3. The original number.

The livery of all coaches was dark green, but this is being changed to cream and green. Vehicles upgraded to 140 km/h are also allowed to work into Belgium, the Netherlands and Germany.

All vehicles were built by Wegmann and are 26.1 m. in length.

A3B9 OPEN COMPOSITE

Accommodation: 24/72 2T.
Max Speed: 140 km/h.

To be converted to open second.

50 82 32-40 417-0	50 82 32-40 417-0	2167	
50 82 32-40 418-8	50 82 32-40 418-8	2168	

B12 OPEN SECOND

Accommodation: –/96 2T.
Max Speed: 120 or 140 km/h.

r Refurbished with asbestos removed.
* Converted from A3B9 (CO).

50 82 22-10 331-1	50 82 22-10 331-1	2101	
50 82 22-10 332-9	50 82 22-40 432-1	2102	r
50 82 22-40 433-9	50 82 22-10 333-7	2103	r
50 82 22-10 334-5	50 82 22-10 334-5	2104	
50 82 22-40 435-4	50 82 22-10 335-2	2105	
50 82 22-40 436-2	50 82 22-10 336-0	2106	r
50 82 22-10 337-8	50 82 22-10 337-8	2107	
50 82 22-40 438-8	50 82 22-10 338-6	2108	r
50 82 22-10 339-4	50 82 22-10 339-4	2109	
50 82 22-40 440-4	50 82 22-10 340-2	2110	r
50 82 22-10 341-0	50 82 22-10 341-0	2111	
50 82 22-10 342-8	50 82 22-10 342-8	2112	
50 82 22-10 343-6	50 82 22-10 343-6	2113	
50 82 22-10 344-4	50 82 22-40 444-6	2114	r
50 82 22-40 445-3	50 82 22-40 445-3	2115	r
50 82 22-10 346-9	50 82 22-10 346-9	2116	

50 82 22-40 447-9	50 82 22-10 347-7	2117	r
50 82 22-10 348-5	50 82 22-10 348-5	2118	
50 82 22-10 349-3	50 82 22-10 349-3	2119	
50 82 22-40 450-3	50 82 22-10 350-1	2120	r
50 82 22-10 351-9	50 82 22-10 351-9	2121	
50 82 22-10 352-7	50 82 22-10 352-7	2122	
50 82 22-10 353-5	50 82 22-10 353-5	2123	
50 82 22-10 354-3	50 82 22-10 354-3	2124	r
50 82 22-10 355-0	50 82 22-10 355-0	2125	
50 82 22-40 456-0	50 82 22-40 456-0	2126	r
50 82 22-40 457-8	50 82 22-40 457-8	2127	
50 82 22-40 458-6	50 82 22-40 458-6	2128	r
50 82 22-10 359-2	50 82 22-10 359-2	2129	
50 82 22-40 460-2	50 82 22-40 460-2	2130	
50 82 22-40 461-0	50 82 22-10 361-8	2131	r
50 82 22-10 362-6	50 82 22-40 462-8	2132	r
50 82 22-10 363-4	50 82 22-40 463-6	2133	r
50 82 22-10 364-2	50 82 22-40 464-4	2134	r
50 82 22-40 465-1	50 82 22-40 465-1	2135	r
50 82 22-40 466-9	50 82 22-40 466-9	2136	r
50 82 22-40 467-7	50 82 22-40 467-7	2161	r*
50 82 22-10 368-3	50 82 22-10 368-3	2162	r*
50 82 22-40 469-3	50 82 22-10 369-1	2163	r*
50 82 22-40 470-1	50 82 22-10 370-9	2166	r*
50 82 22-40 471-9	50 82 22-40 471-9	2169	r*
50 82 22-40 472-7	50 82 22-40 472-7	2137	r*
50 82 22-10 373-3	50 82 22-40 473-5	2138	r*
50 82 22-40 474-3	50 82 32-40 414-7	2164	*
50 82 22-40 475-0	50 82 32-40 415-4	2165	r*

A3B6D (A6B3D§)   BRAKE OPEN COMPOSITE

All converted from B9D (BSO).

Accommodation: 24/48 1T (48/24 1T*).
Max Speed: 120 or 140 km/h.

§ Centre compartment is first instead of end compartment.
r Refurbished with asbestos removed.

50 82 81-40 480-8	50 82 81-10 380-6	2189	r§
50 82 81-10 381-4	50 82 81-10 381-4	2191	r
50 82 81-40 482-4	50 82 81-40 482-4	2193	r
50 82 81-40 483-2	50 82 81-40 483-2	2183	r
50 82 81-40 484-0	50 82 81-40 484-0	2184	r
50 82 81-40 485-7	50 82 81-40 485-7	2186	r§
50 82 81-40 486-5	50 82 81-40 486-5	2187	
50 82 81-40 487-3	50 82 81-40 487-3	2188	r
50 82 81-10 388-9	50 82 82-10 390-4	2190	r
50 82 81-10 389-7	50 82 82-10 392-0	2192	r
50 82 81-40 491-5	50 82 82-10 391-2	2181	
50 82 81-10 393-9	50 82 82-10 393-8	2182	
50 82 81-10 394-6	50 82 82-10 394-6	2185	

PRESERVED LOCOS & MULTIPLE UNITS

Number	Type	Built	Status	Location
105	1A – A1 DMMU	1949	MR	GAR. Luxembourg depot
151	A – 1 DMMU	1951	MA	Fond de Gras
455	C dh	1963	MS	CFL. Luxembourg depot
2001	B dh	1957	MS	CFL. Luxembourg depot
5519	2 – 10 – 0	1947	MA	CFL. Luxembourg depot

For status codes see SNCB section.
For society and railway abbreviations see the "Museums and Museum Lines" section.

MUSEUMS & MUSEUM LINES

Preservation in the three Benelux countries for many years was only represented by the offical collections in Belgium and the Netherlands. Then came the preservation boom of the late 1960s and it has really taken off since then. Unfortunately the Benelux countries were some of the first in Europe to eliminate main line steam so that steam preservation has been mostly of Industrial types or of locos obtained from other countries - notably Germany. Like other countries on the European mainland, museum line operations tend to be at weekends only but there are notable exceptions with some lines having daily trains in the peak summer months. All railways/tramways are standard gauge (1435 mm) unless otherwise shown. Two museum lines have closed down in recent years and another has relocated. Those that have closed are the MSTB at Vilvoorde and Li Tremleu at Trembleur. The Zolder line has relocate.

BELGIUM.

As – Eisden 6km.

Limburgse Stoomvereniging. LSV. This is the former Zolder operation relocated. Besides the 'main line' operation there is also a short narrow gauge mining line. Operates Sundays June – August with steam usually operating in July and August. Santa trains run in November.
7 steam and other stock.

Brussels.

Musée Nationale des Chemins de Fer/Museum van de Spoorwegen. The National Railway Museum is located in Brussels Nord station, the entrance being off the booking hall. Only one loco is present, the others in the collection being stored at Leuven until suitable premises can be found. There are many models and photos etc. explaining the development of railways in Belgium. Open Monday – Friday and first Saturday of the month if it is not a holiday. 09.00 – 16.30.

Brussels.

Musée du Transport Urbain Bruxellois. MTUB. This tram and bus museum is located in the suburb of Woluwe St. Pierre at the old depot there. Access is by trams 39 or 44 and buses 36 or 42. Tourist services operate over part of route 44. Open on Saturdays, Sundays and holidays April-September. 13.30 – 19.00.
More than 40 trams/buses.

Ciney – Spontin. 9 km.

Patrimoine Ferroviaire Touristique. PFT. A relatively new organisation but a very active one that is growing at a fast rate. It has preserved many SNCB diesel locos and railcars and imported a working steam loco from Poland now renumbered '26.101'. Most stock is kept at Schaerbeek depot.
1 steam, 6 diesels, 1 EMU, 5 DMU.

Dendermonde – Puurs. 14 km.

Stoomspoorlijn Dendermonde – Puurs. SDP. Operates over closed NMBS line. Operates on Sundays in July and August with some extra operating days on certain Saturdays and holidays. Mixed steam and diesel operation.
Revised stock totals 6 steam, 2 diesel, 1 diesel railcar.

Edegem.

Antwerps Tram en Autobusmuseum. This is part of the AMUTRA organisation. Access by bus 32 from Antwerpen or Berchem stations or trams 7 and 15 from Antwerpen. The museum is located in the Fort V recreational park and is open weekends and holidays Easter to end of October. 14.00 – 18.00.
More than 25 trams and buses.

Erezee – Dochamps. 12 km.

1000 mm. Tramway Touristique de l'Aisne. TTA. An interesting preserved tramway deep in the Ardennes and rather inaccessible. The operating base is Pont D'Erezee which is not on the railway network. Public transport details are not known. Operates Sundays and holidays April – September and Mondays excepted mid-July – end of August.
3 steam, 3 trams.

Essen Wildert.

De Bakkersmolen. Historic windmill and bakery with 600 mm railway circuit.
3 steam, 1 diesel.

Eupen – Raeren – Bullingen/Trois Ponts. 65 km!

Vennbahn. This line straddles the German border area and was of strategic importance until quite recently. Operates on Sundays and Belgian/German holidays 30th April – 30th October. Steam loco used on first weekend of each month operating the first Saturday to Trois Ponts and the first Sunday to Bullingen. Eupen depart 10.00. Belgian and DR diesel locos used at other times. A German offshoot now provides a connecting shuttle from Stolberg using ex ÖBB DMUs.

Haine St. Pierre.

The old SNCB depot here (adjacent to La Louvière Sud station) is now closed and being used to store and restore SNCB and private museum line stock. SNCB has many carriages and wagons here but the locos present are mostly from the Mariembourg collection. Not normally open to the public.
5 – 7 steam, 2 EMUs.

Kinkempois.

ATF Kinkempois. This is a regional railway museum located at the SNCB depot where the staff have restored diesel 6041.

Leuven.

Former NMBS depot and workshop. Most of the locomotives and rolling stock belonging to the National Collection are housed here. The premises are classed as a workshop and are not open to the public. Restoration work is carried out here. However, recognising the public interest in the collection, there are usually open days several times a year especially in early September.
19 steam, 2 diesels, 2 EMUs, 3 DMUs.

Liège.

Musée des Transports en commun du pays de Liège. A collection of trams and buses. The museum is located at Rue Richard Heintz, 9 and is on bus routes 4, 26. 28 and 31. Open weekends and holidays April – mid October.

Lobbes – Thuin. 5 km.

1000 mm. Association pour la Sauvegarde du Vicinal. ASVi. A tramway operation over a scenic cross country SNCV route. Operates Sunday and holiday afternoons 1st May – 16th October in 1994. SNCB excursion ticket 102 gets you there. First departure is 13.25 from Lobbes. The depot is believed to be at Anderlues.
Trams.

Maldegem.

600 mm and 1435 mm. Stoom Centrum Maldegem. SCM. A museum has been established alongside the old station at Maldegem and a 2 km narrow gauge line constructed. The society now also operates over the SNCB line to Eeklo (10 km). The museum is open daily July and August and Sundays and holidays 1st May – 30th September, 10.00 – 17.00. Trains operate Sundays and holidays 1st May – 30th September. Traction engines and agricultural equipment are also present.
4 steam, 3 diesel, 1 battery electric (600 mm): 3 steam, 1 diesel railcar (1435 mm).

Mariembourg.
Mariembourg – Chimay – Momignies. 29 km.
Mariembourg – Treignes. 14 km.
Dinant – Heer Agimont – Givet. 22 km.

Chemin de Fer à Vapeur des Trois Vallées (CFV3V). The CFV3V has expanded considerably in the last few years. Its main base remains Mariembourg from where operations now reach Momignies and even sometimes to Anor in France. At the other end of the system at Treignes a new locomotive and rolling stock museum has been erected and opened its doors in May 1994. Locos are kept at Treignes, Mariembourg, Haine St. Pierre and Heer Agimont. This last outpost is for working along

the scenic valley line to Givet in France. In early 1994 two former 2 – 10 – 0s arrived on the CFV3V and a Polish TSKt48 is expected. Operating days are Saturdays, Sundays and holidays 2nd April – 30th October and daily Mariembourg – Treignes July and August and on Fridays also between Dinant and Givet.
27 steam, 7 diesels, 11 diesel railcars.

Mechelen.

De Mijlpaal. Regional railway museum believed to be located in part of the NMBS workshops.
1 electric, 1 EMU.

Oostende.

TTO Nordzee. Excursions operate from time to time over the coastal tramway system using vintage stock.

Rebecq – Rognon. 3 km.

600 mm. Rail Rebecq – Rognon. RRR. Located near Tubize from where there is an infrequent bus service or a 45 minute walk. The line serves a pleasant area along the River Senne. Operates Sundays and holidays May – September.
3 steam, 3 diesel.

Schepdaal.

600, 1000. 1435 mm. Association pour le Musée du Tramway. AMUTRA. A large collection of tramway equipment which includes 3 steam locos. Located 13 km from Brussels, access is by bus N Brussels – Ninove. Open Sundays and holidays Easter – October and also Saturdays in July and August, 14.00 – 18.00.
3 steam, 3 diesel railcars, many trams.

Sprimont.

600 mm. Chemin de Fer de Sprimont. CFS. This line is built on the trackbed of a former SNCV line and uses old mining diesel locos. Operates first and third Sundays of the month May – September from 14.00. Festival on the last weekend of August. Public transport access is believed to be by bus from Poulseur – Trooz. Nearest main towns are Liège and Spa.
6 diesels.

NETHERLANDS

Amsterdam.

Electrische Museumtramlijn. Amsterdam has a large collection of museum trams and trailers and operates over the city network. Most of the stock is at the Karpennreg depot but some may also be found at Havenstraat depot.
33 trams, 20 trailers, 2 electric locomotives, 5 diesel locomotives and numerous other tramway type equipment.

Apeldoorn – Dieren. 22 km.

Veluwsche Stoomtrein Maatschappij. VSM. Uses mostly former DB/DR locos. Operates over a closed NS branch line on which the depot is located at Beekbergen. Main operating days are Mondays – Fridays and Sundays in July and August. Uses mostly former DB locos.
10 steam, 4 diesel, 1 diesel railcar.

Barger Compascuum. 1 km.

700 mm. Eerste Drentse Vereniging van Stoomliefhebbers EDS. This operation is in the National Veenpark and a short train journey is made through the old village. This Moorland Park is open every day from April to October. The train rides are included in the entrance fee.
2 steam, 10 diesels.

Beverwijk. 9 km.

Hoogovens Excursietrein. This is a steam hauled excursion train around the vast steelworks covering 18 kms return journey which takes some 2 hours. Photo stops are made on the journey. Departure is from Beverwijk station at 10.45 on the last Sunday of the month May to September.
2 steam. (Plus all the industrial diesels in the steelworks!).

Erica.

700 mm. Industrieel Smalspoormuseum te Erica. A rather new museum about which little is known except the rolling stock.
1 steam, 46 diesels, 3 electrics.

Goes – Oudelande. 16 km.

Stoomtram Goes – Borsele. SGB. This line uses a former NS freight line. The depot is located at Goes station and is in fact the old NS depot. In July and August the line operates daily except Saturdays. Early and late operations are normally Sundays only but in September there is usually an 'Historic Weekend' (10/11 September in 1994) when extra attractions are laid on. On Wednesday evenings in July and August there is a wine and dine train departing Goes at 19.00 with a return arrival at 22.00.
4 steam, 3 diesel.

Haaksbergen – Boekelo. 7 km.

Museum Buurt Spoonrveg. MBS. The depot is located at Haaksbergen which is 9 km from Enschede and can be accessed by TET buses 53, 57, 58 from Hengelo and GVM buses 20, 21, 27 from Enschede. Operates Sundays June – September and Wednesdays and Thursday in July and August plus other odd days. Three round trips normally operate departing Haaksbergen at 11.30, 13.30 and 15.30.
5 steam, 7 diesels, 2 DMUs.

Den Haag.

Haagse Tram Museum. HTM. Museum trams operate on certain Saturdays or Sundays in the summer.

Hoorn – Medemblik. 20 km.

Stoomtram Hoorn – Medemblik. SHM. This line is well established and a visit is recommended. The depot is adjacent to Hoorn NS station. NS day trip tickets can be purchased if a railrover is not being used. It is possible to do a train-boat-train circular journey. During July/August operation is daily whilst at other times between May and September there are no trains on Mondays. This line has also moved into the wine and dine market and runs the 'Candle Light Express' on Friday and Saturday evenings departing at 18.15 and returning at 22.50.
8 steam, 4 diesels, 1 DMU.

De Punt – Port Zelande 5 km.

1067 mm. Recreatif Toeristische Museumtramlijn. Goedereede. This is the old RTM setup relocated from Hellevoetsluis which has not operated for some 6 years but should restart services this year.
3 steam, 4 diesel railcars, 1 diesel.

Kaatsheuvel. 1.5 km.

600 mm. Efteling Stoomtrein Maatschaapij. This is a steam operation in a vast amusement park close to Tilburg. The park is open and trains run each day April to October between 10.00 – 18.00.
4 steam.

Rotterdam.

Rotterdamse Elektrische Tramwegmaatschappij. RET. During the summer the Stichting Brabant Rail have been running their steam tram from Centraal station to Willemsplein usually hourly between 10.00 and 15.00. Additionally Tramweg Stichting has preserved several Rotterdam trams and these may be used on sightseeing trips almost at anytime.

Rotterdam.

Stoom Stichting Nederland. SSN. This society's depot is located at Spaanse Polder, Giessenweg. Take tram RET 1/6/8 from Rotterdam or even the metro to Marconiplein or alternatively bus RET 38 from Schiedam to Franselaan. The SSN does not have a museum line but is able to run its locos several times each year on excursion trains over the NS. Most of the locos are former DB ones. The depot is normally open each Saturday 10.00 – 17.00.
8 steam, 1 diesel.

Schin op Geul – Simpelveld – Kerkrade. ? km.

Zuid Limburgsche Stoomtrein Maatschappi, ZLSM. This line was expected to start operations in 1994 using Simpelveld as its base. One diesel loco so far with some steam locos expected from Sweden.

Utrecht.

Nederlands Spoorweg Museum, Maliebaanstation, Johan van Oldenbarneveldtlaan 6. The NS museum was considerably enlarged for the 1987 NS celebrations and work has continued since then to further improve the site. Open Tuesday – Saturday 10.00 – 17.00 and Sundays 13.00 – 17.00. Access used to be by bus 3 from Utrecht CS to Rubenslaan but this may have changed.
15 steam, 6 diesel, 4 EMUs, 4 DMUs and trams.

Valkenburg, Zuid Holland.

This is the new location for Nederlandse Smalspoorweg Stichting, formally at Katwijk. The extent of their new operating line is not known but a completely new depot and workshop has been built to house their ever increasing stock. Operates each Saturday June to September.
15 steam, 55 diesels (700, 900 mm gauges).

LUXEMBOURG.

Luxembourg.

CFL Depot. Staff here have restored CFL 5519 (2 – 10 – 0) and it is used on excursions from time to time. Two diesel locos are also preserved here.
1 steam, 2 diesels.

Luxembourg.

CFL Depot. Groupement des Amis du Rail. GAR. This society is also based at the CFL Depot and has a former ÖBB Class 52 2 – 10 – 0 and a CFL diesel railcar.

Rodange. 5 km.

Association des Musée et Tourisme Ferroviaires. AMTF. The depot for this line is at Fond de Gras. Access to the line is Rodange station and a mile walk to Bois de Rodange where the museum line station is located. Operations are on Sundays and holidays May to September. Usually three trips during the afternoon are made by the steam train and a DMU is also used if another steam loco is not available for the second train or traffic is light.
7 steam, 2 diesel, 1 DMU.

SNCB DEPOT CODES

The SNCB has used codes for depots & stabling points for many years dating back to the days of the telegraph system. These telegraph codes are still in use today as official abbreviations. However on locomotives the allocation is stencilled on in full on the main frame somewhere below the cab. EMUs and DMUs do not normally carry their allocations but some of the codes will be found on them against repair data etc.

ATH	Ath	FSN	St. Niklaas
FAZ	Salzinnes Works(Namur)	FSR	Schaarbeek Diesel
FBMZ	Brussels Midi/Zuid	FSRE	Schaarbeek Electric
FCL	Châtelet	FTM	Tamines
FCR	Charleroi Sud	FTR	Turnhout
FDD	Denderleeuw	FTY	Tournai
FDK	De Panne	FVS	Visé
FDN	Oudenarde	FVY	Gouvy
FDR	Dendermonde	FWO	Wondelgem
FEO	Ronet (Namur)	GMN	Montzen
FF	Forest-Vorst	GNS	Antwerpen Oost
FGH	St. Ghislain	GT	Haine St. Pierre
FGRA	Geraardsbergen	GWK	Welkenraedt
FGSP	Gent St. Pieters	LBC	Bascoup
FHS	Hasselt	LJ	Jemelle
FKR	Merelbeke (Gent)	LK	Kortrijk
FL	Liège Guillemins	LL	Aarlon
FLS	Aalst	LML	Mol
FLV	Leuven	LNC	Monceau (Charleroi)
FM	Mechelen Works	LRB	Libramont
FMS	Mons	LSL	Liers
FN	Antwerpen Centraal	LT	Ottignies
FNDM	Antwerpen Dam	LY	Huy
FNND	Antwerpen Noord	MBX	Bertrix
FNR	Namur	MGR	Angleur
FNZG	Antwerpen Schijnpoort	MKM	Stockem (Arlon)
FR	Brugge	MUT	Latour
FRST	Aarschot	NK	Kinkempois (Liège)
FSD	Oostende		

SNCB & NS LIVERY CODES

The following livery codes are used in this book. Where no code is shown against the individual vehicle, it is assumed that NS locomotives are yellow & grey, NS coaching stock & multiple units are plain yellow, and Belgian vehicles are olive green. Where two colours are shown, the first colour mentioned is the colour on the lower half of the body.

B Benelux push-pull livery (yellow & bordeaux red).
D SNCB/NMBS diesel railcar livery (red & yellow).
E Eurostar. White with dark blue window band roof and yellow bodysides.
G Original green livery.
I NS Intercity livery (yellow & blue).
N Non-standard livery (refer to text).
O Orange & grey.
P Post office red (SNCB/NMBS), yellow/red (NS).
R Bordeaux red (SNCB/NMBS), raspberry red (NS Cargo).
S New SNCB/NMBS 'break' unit livery. Silver with red and blue.
U Unpainted stainless steel with coloured stripe.
X Old Benelux push-pull livery. Dark blue with yellow stripe.
Y Blue lower bodyside & yellow upper bodyside.
W White (new SNCB/NMBS DMU livery).